Soft Furnishings for the Home

AURA
EDITIONS

Editor: Alison Wormleighton
Designer: Caroline Dewing

Published by Aura Editions
2 Derby Road, Greenford, Middlesex

Produced by Marshall Cavendish Books Limited
58 Old Compton Street, London W1V 5PA

© Marshall Cavendish Limited 1985

ISBN 0 86307 283 6

Typesetting and make-up by Quadraset Limited,
Midsomer Norton, Bath, Avon

Printed and bound by
Grafiche Editoriali Padane S.p.A., Cremona, Italy

Contents

Introduction

The soft furnishings in your home—curtains, cushions, bed and table linen and other accessories made from fabric—play an important role in interior design. They soften the bare bones of walls and woodwork, and the style of fabric used sets the style of a room: jazzy, modern prints in a bright, young living room; soft floral designs to create a cottagey atmosphere; textured fabrics in subdued colours for a classical, elegant style. As well as being functional, soft furnishings are one of the easiest elements in a room to change, as they are neither expensive nor disruptive to replace.

In the bedroom, new curtains and bed linen can completely alter the style and colouring of the room. And once you have bought or made the new furnishings, the transformation takes no more than half an hour! But the bedroom is not the only room which will benefit from carefully selected soft furnishings.

In the living room you can change the feel of the room to suit the seasons. Heavy velvet curtains and dark loose covers on the sofa or armchairs create a warm and inviting atmosphere, perfect for winter. Then, in the summer, you can change the mood with soft lacy nets at the window and pale pastel covers on the seating, a room for cool respite from the summer sun. In the dining room you could even go so far as to change some of your soft furnishings to suit the time of day: pretty pastel prints for a spring-fresh breakfast all year round; cheerful gingham for a traditional farmhouse kitchen atmosphere at lunchtime; and crisp white linen to enhance the menu when guests come to dinner.

All kinds of transformations are possible, and of course sewing some or all of your soft furnishings yourself is a great economy. Home sewing also gives you tremendous scope and flexibility. You can choose from vast ranges of fabrics, and create a totally individual look. Indeed, the choice of fabrics is always increasing, but manufacturers have created an easy way out by creating ranges of fabrics designed to co-ordinate with wallpapers. Some even go so far as to recommend carpets and paint colours, so that you can achieve a total look with a minimum of worry. As well as the more necessary and functional basics of décor, such as curtains and linen, there are other accessories which make a statement about decorative style. Soft, pleated fabric lampshades, padded picture frames, piles of cushions and frilled blinds and tie-backs are some of the ingredients of the total fabric look which has become so popular.

To create your chosen style you have to master a few basic skills. The projects in this book not only give a thorough grounding in the basics, but take you on to a more advanced level, for example, using and designing appliqué patterns to embellish soft furnishings. Once you've learnt the basics you can go on to develop your own projects. The book also acts as an introduction to more specialized skills like upholstery and lampshade making. Once you have practised the techniques in the projects here you will be well on the way to understanding the skills involved in these hobbies.

CHAPTER 1

Cushy number

Cushions are a marvellous way to introduce patterns and
textures to a room. Great favourites with interior designers,
they add interest and softness as well as extra comfort.

Cushions come in all shapes and sizes, from square, boxy cushions with neat piping outlining the seams, to soft, feathery cushions in a fluffy cascade of frills and bows.

Since the size of cushions is generally small in comparison to the whole room, they give an opportunity to add splashes of colour and texture which might become too dominant if the same fabrics were used in larger areas—as curtains or upholstery, for example.

Cushions are also a delightful way to show off crafts—needlepoint, embroidery, appliqué or patchwork, for instance. Again, the relatively small size of cushions makes them an ideal project for a novice at the craft.

Cushions for colour

Your choice of colours, patterns and textures is limited only by the ranges of fabrics and yarns available. For a smart, co-ordinated look, use the same fabrics as curtains or lampshades. Or match the cushions to the wallcovering by using fabric from a 'mix-and-match' range of wallcoverings and fabrics. Cushions which match or tone with either a dominant or a secondary colour in a room are an easy way to 'pull together' a room with a somewhat bewildering mixture of colours and patterns.

If your room is plain-coloured, you can add splashes of interest with cushions in vibrant and primary shades. For a dramatic effect, mass together cushions in strong colours.

For a more restrained, but still exciting look, cover cushions in tones of the same colour, for example, shades of blue, from navy to ice-blue, or red tones, from maroon to pale pink.

Patterns and textures

Choose fabrics to fit in with the style and furnishings you already have. In a country-style room, with stripped pine furniture and china plates displayed on the sideboard, flower print cottons or ginghams are a good choice. However, with reproduction or antique furniture, velvets and brocades give a more formal effect.

Cotton furnishing fabrics are one of the best choices for covers. Cotton is an easy fabric to work with, particularly if you are piping the cushions or adding frills, and it is washable, an important factor when making cushions which will be subject to a lot of wear. Cotton fabrics are also available in a wide choice of colours and patterns for coordinated effects.

Floral-patterned cushions are particularly attractive with wooden furnishings: pale, modern prints with pine; more formal, darker prints with mahogany; and bright, bold prints with painted furniture. Crisp cottons in a geometric print or trellis pattern look good with the rounded, uneven shapes of cane and bamboo furniture. And lacy, textured cushions make a lovely contrast to the regular, smooth finish of a brass bedhead.

Inside and out

The filling you choose for a cushion may depend on the use it will have. Soft, feather-filled cushions make a delightful, frothy display at the head of a bed. Firmer cushions, tightly filled with foam chips, may be a better choice on a sofa or window seat, where you want the cushions to keep their shape. In an armchair, feather- or acrylic-filled cushions will mould to your body better.

For the seat of a dining chair, or a cushion to fit the top of a low pine chest, use a slab of foam, shaped to fit. Fit the cover tightly over the cushions.

For large floor cushions, polystyrene granules fulfil a double role: they mould to fit the body, but don't squash down, so they give continued support.

It is a good idea to make cushion covers removable for washing. If you are making the cushion pad, enclose the filling in a feather-proof cover, then make a removable cover. It may be stitched by hand, which gives a neat, unobtrusive finish, but involves work unpicking and re-stitching the seam each time you wash the cushion. A zip set into the back of the cushion is convenient and neat, but adds to the cost of making it. Poppers, press stud tapes and hook-and-eye tapes are a cheaper finish. One of the simplest ways to make a cover which is easily removable is to make a tuck-in flap at the back, like the 'housewife' style closure on a pillowcase.

All sorts of shapes

There is no need to stick to square-shaped cushions. Mix together square and round cushions for both comfort and

Cushions provide a splendid opportunity to show off favourite needlecrafts, such as appliqué and shadow work.

a good looking display. Larger bolster-shaped cushions can be used on their own, for example along the back of a single bed in a teenager's bedroom, or in a bedsitting room to turn the bed into a sofa by day. Smaller bolster shapes mix well with round and square cushions. Make a long, tube-shaped cover and gather the ends to make shapes like soft Christmas crackers.

Cushions can also be made in novelty shapes. Make cushions the shape of fruit or vegetables and pile them on a bench in a country kitchen. Animal-shaped cushions can double as toys in a child's bedroom. Or choose heart-shaped cushions to adorn a romantic bedroom— then add heart-shaped accessories.

7

When it comes to floor cushions, you can really go to town with novelty effects. Make a sag bag to look like a huge, squashy beach ball, in brightly coloured canvas, or make cushions from blocks of foam in the shape of liquorice allsorts.

A long snake which can be coiled up or snaked around the room provides an endless variety of seating arrangements.

Decorative detail

If you enjoy hand sewing or decorative stitching, cushions are an ideal place to show off your skills. Patchwork is an effective way to combine fabrics in different colours and patterns to make attractive, decorative covers.

Appliqué is another way of combining different patterns, and you can create pretty, pictorial effects by appliquéing shades of blue, green and brown to make landscapes, or floral fabrics to make big bunches of flowers. In a child's room why not go to town with bold, alphabet cushions, or favourite story-book characters in appliqué?

The range of embroidered designs available is growing all the time. Choose traditional, Italian Florentine needlepoint in rich colours for a grand sitting room; floral needlepoint designs for a window seat looking out on to the garden; or old-fashioned cross-stitch patterns for a farmhouse-style kitchen.

For a room with a subdued colour scheme, textured needlepoint, combining different stitches in the same colour, will be more in harmony.

Knitted or crocheted squares or circles can also be made up into cushions. Knitted pictures, a patchwork of crocheted granny squares, textured finishes with mixed yarns and stitches—all have their place.

Satin-covered bolsters trimmed with tassels add elegance to a bedroom.

Kitchen chair cushions

Brighten up those hard, wooden kitchen chairs with a set of colourful cushions. In smart cotton fabric, with neat piped edges, they are held in place on the seats with ties that form bows round the back chair struts. Make them up to match your tablecloth and napkins, or to tone in with your kitchen curtains or blind.

Before you begin

When choosing a fabric for kitchen chair cushions, bear in mind that these covers need to withstand the wear and tear of meal times and will probably need to be washed more often than sofa cushions. A cotton or cotton mix is the best type of fabric to use as it is hardwearing and washes well. Another material that

would be suitable for kitchen chair cushions is PVC. This man-made fabric is very strong with a shiny surface and cotton back. It can easily be wiped clean or washed by hand and it does not need to be ironed.

When buying your fabric, always pick the best quality you can afford. Avoid large patterns which can be wasteful to match on cushions and choose smaller prints which will be more economical. Before you buy, look at the fabric in daylight, as well as in the artificial light of the shop, as the colours can alter dramatically. It is best to test a piece in the room where it is to be used. Do make sure that you buy enough for the complete job; if you need to buy more, the colours may

not match, as dyes do vary from length to length.

If you are using inner covers, make them in calico, cambric or lining, or use old sheets. To achieve really professional results, make the inner cover first and when making the main cover, try it on the cushion pad before stitching by machine. This way you can make any necessary adjustments to achieve a perfect fit.

Foam

Synthetic foam is the best filling for hard-wearing square-shaped cushions. This type of foam is made in various densities, which depend on the amount of air incorporated during manufacture. The higher the weight, the more solid the foam will be. For a simple cushion a low-density, plain foam is quite sufficient.

If you wish, you can cover the foam with an inner cover. When the foam starts to crumble, after years of use, you can throw the complete cushion pad away and replace it.

Foam can be bought in a variety of thicknesses from about 6mm upwards and generally comes in large sheets which can be cut to the correct size in the shop.

Piping cord

Piping cord is sold in different thickness, from No. 00 to No. 6. Pick one that is suitable for the job; generally you should use a No. 4 cord for cushions unless they are large or very small.

Fasteners

Cushions can be fastened in a variety of ways: with zips, velcro, hooks and eyes, press fasteners, press fastening tape or by simply stitching the two open edges together. If the cushions are to go in the kitchen and therefore will be washed more often than usual, insert a fastening

that has a long life and is easily undone, such as a zip. It provides a neat finish and if set into the cushion base is also invisible. Buy a zip the correct length for the cushion, so that the cushion pad can be removed easily without causing the zip too much strain. A base zip will be stitched centrally into a horizontal seam, so allow about 5cm at each end of the seam then measure the centre portion for the zip length. Make sure that you buy the correct weight: for cotton fabric or PVC, a dress-making zip will be suitable.

Materials

☐ 2m × 120cm wide main cover fabric for three cushions
☐ 1m contrasting fabric for the piping
☐ Matching zip
☐ No. 4 piping cord
☐ Foam for filling
☐ Matching thread
☐ Paper for template
☐ Felt-tip pen
☐ Fabric for inner cover, optional

Making-up instructions

1 Making the pattern

To make a template for the cushion, cut a

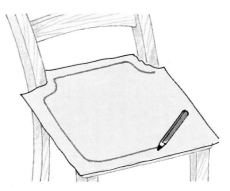

piece of paper—this can be newspaper, tracing paper or brown paper—into the general shape of the chair seat. Place the

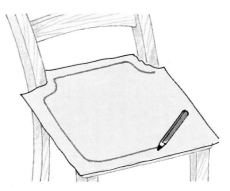

Plain fabrics, floral prints and small graphic patterns in bright colours in cotton or PVC look pretty and cheerful in kitchens.

paper on the chair, aligning one straight edge with the back edge of the chair.

Using a felt-tip pen, mark round the outline of the chair. Remove the paper from the chair and cut round the marked line. Replace the template on the chair and check that it fits. Mark the positions of the back ties at the two back chair struts.

2 Calculating the fabric

Mark out the width of the chosen fabric on a table or floor. Position your template inside this area and see how many you can cut from the fabric width; you will need two pieces for each cushion. Place the template parallel with the selvedge and add a 1.5cm seam allowance all round.

The cushion gusset will be cut on the bias. If possible, allow for sufficient fabric to make the correct length of the gusset without a join. For the length, measure round the outer edge of the template, adding 3cm for the seam allowance. The width for kitchen cushions should be about 4cm, plus a 1.5cm seam allowance on each side. Also buy 50cm of plain fabric for the piping.

3 Cutting the foam

Cut the foam 6mm larger than the

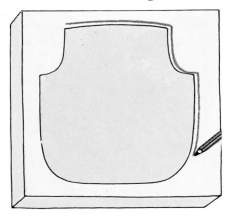

template all round, so that it will fit snugly into the sides and corners of the cover, pushing out any fabric wrinkles. Lay the template on the foam and, using a felt-tip pen, mark round, adding the extra 6mm.

Cut the foam with a long-bladed serrated knife, such as a bread or craft knife. Hold the knife at a 45-degree angle and make shallow downward cuts in the foam, drawing the knife along the marked line. Make several cuts to get through the foam.

4 Cutting out the fabric

For the cushion top, place the template on the wrong side of the fabric and pin in place. Cut out, adding a 1.5cm seam allowance all round.

Divide the template into two halves widthways, because the zip will be inserted in the cushion base. Place the two pieces on the wrong side of the fabric, matching edges, and then move them 3cm apart to allow for the zip seam. Cut out the two pieces.

Cut out the gusset on the bias. If possible, cut one continuous length.

For the piping, cut out 4cm wide strips on the fabric bias, which when stitched together will make twice the gusset length.

To find the bias, fold the fabric diagonally so that the selvedge matches the straight of grain. Cut along the fold line and cut all strips parallel to the cut edge.

5 Inserting the zip

Before stitching the cover together, insert the zip. Pin, tack and stitch the two base pieces with right sides together for about 5cm from each end of the seam. Press the seam open.

Pin the closed zip behind the opening with the teeth lying face up under the pressed, open seam. Tack and stitch the zip in place. Partially open the zip and

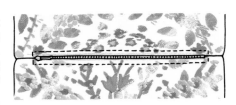

continue to make up the cushion. If the zip is closed, you will not be able to turn the finished cushion right side out!

For ties, cut out two 3cm wide strips, each about 60cm long. Fold each tie in half lengthways, right side inwards. Pin, tack and stitch, taking a 5mm wide seam allowance and leaving the ends open. Trim and turn right side out. Press the seam to the back. Turn in the ends and slipstitch.

6 Joining bias strips

Stitch the bias strips together to make up the required length. All seams should be made on the straight of grain. Place two strips with right sides together with the ends matching. Slide the top strip 1.5cm towards the bottom strip. Stitch together by machine 1.5cm from the edge.

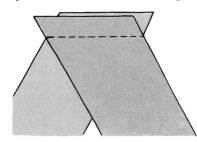

7 Preparing fabric for piping

Press the seams open and trim off the corners so that the seam allowances are level with the side edges.

8 Making the piping

Trim one end of the strip on the straight of grain. Fold the strip evenly in half with wrong sides together round the piping

cord, with the cord extending beyond the end of the strip. Pin, tack and stitch by machine as close to the piping as possible, using the zipper foot and gently pulling the fabric strip as you stitch.

9 Mounting piping on cushion top
Starting on the right side of the cushion top at the straight back edge, pin and tack the piping in place with the raw edges matching. At each corner, clip into the seam allowance of the piping fabric.

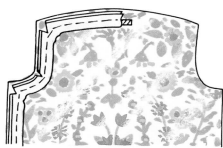

10 Joining piping cord
To join the ends, unpick the stitching along the piping fabric for 5cm in each direction and join the ends of the fabric with a diagonal seam.

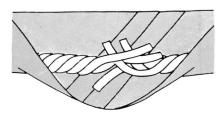

To join the cord, unwind the piping cord from each end, and cut out one strand from one side and two strands from the opposite side. Rewind the cord and bind together.

Fold the piping fabric evenly in half over the join; pin, tack and stitch.

11 Positioning ties
Fold each tie evenly in half and place on the cushion base at the marked positions, over the seamline.

12 Mounting piping on cushion base
Position the covered piping cord round the cushion base over the ties. Pin and tack in place.

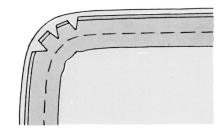

13 Joining the cushion pieces
Position the gusset round the cushion top, with right sides together and raw edges matching. Pin, tack and stitch in place over the piping tacking line. Join the gusset ends together at centre back edge to fit. Place the cushion base to the opposite edge of the gusset; pin, tack and stitch in place in the same way. Trim the seams.

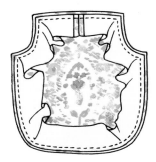

14 Making an inner cover
If you are using an inner cover, make it in the same way as the main one, omitting zip, piping and ties.

11

Square cushion covers

Cushions are a quick and easy way to add individual touches to your home. A plain room can be enhanced by a stylish collection of different design cushions in co-ordinating colours; a set of smart matching piped or flanged cushions adds elegance to a more formal room, while pretty frilled cushions are ideal for a casual room setting or a bedroom.

Before you begin

Select the size of your cushions carefully, and remember a frilled or flanged edge will increase the appearance of the size. The most common sizes for ready-made pads are 35cm, 38cm and 40cm square. Generally, smaller cushions look best on smaller size furniture while they would seem lost on a big sofa, where a larger size is more suitable.

The instructions given are for covers to fit the average 38cm square pad. 1.5cm seam allowances are included throughout. However, it is quite simple to adjust the dimensions to fit a larger or smaller pad by adding or subtracting the required amount of fabric. Styles with edge trims will also need the lengths of the trims adjusted.

Suitable fabrics

Most furnishing fabrics, from textured cotton to linen looks and printed cotton, can be used for cushion covers. Thicker fabrics such as velvet, heavier woollens and repp are more suitable for plain edge or piped covers.

Finer glazed cottons, poplins and satins can be used for most designs.

The covers have zip openings at the centre back for ease of laundering, and it is worthwhile checking whether a fabric is washable.

Checks and stripes

When using checked or striped fabric, the cushions will look more effective if the cover finishes with a whole check or stripe at the outer edges. The lines of a design can also be used as a guide for stitching. If the check or stripe does not match up to the dimensions given, the sizing can be adjusted up to 1cm larger or smaller all round without need to change the size of the pad used.

Cushion pads

Square cushion pads can be purchased in various sizes, 35cm, 38cm and 40cm square being the most readily available. However, should you want a different size, you can easily make your own. Use ticking or feather-proof fabric and feather filling (0.5kg for a 38cm pad) or foam chips (0.75kg for a 38cm pad).

Geometric patterns or small floral prints in soft colours make lovely cushions, particularly in mix-and-match cotton fabrics.

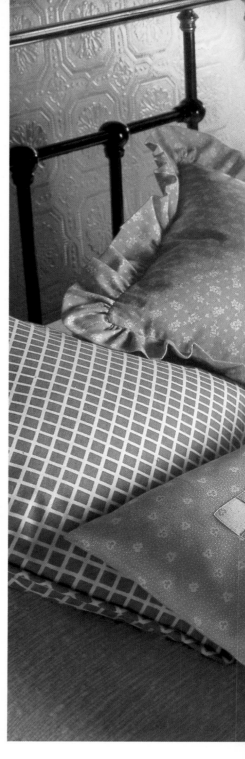

Making a square cushion pad

1 Making the covering

Cut out two pieces to required finished shape plus 1.5cm seam allowance all round. With right sides together, edges level and a small machine stitch, stitch pieces together 1.5cm in from raw edges leaving a 13cm opening along one side.

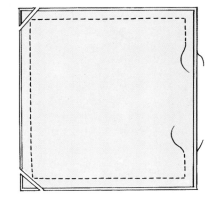

2 Completing and filling the pad

Trim seam allowance at corners and turn right side out. Press seam to edge, and seam allowances to side along opening. Insert filling. With edges level pin or tack edges of opening flat together. Machine stitch along edge to close opening securely.

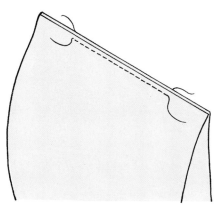

Making a piped cover

Materials

- ☐ 70cm × 120cm wide fabric
- ☐ 160cm × No. 4 piping cord
- ☐ 30cm zip
- ☐ Matching sewing thread

1 Cutting out

Mark out a 42cm square for front; and a piece 42cm × 45cm for back. On remaining fabric mark out bias strips 5cm wide to make one 160cm strip when joined. On check fabrics, position diagonal centre of check centrally along strips. Cut out.

2 Making back opening

Fold back in half with shorter edges level

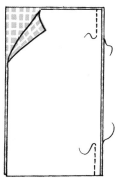

at one side. Cut along fold. Stitch cut edges together 1.5cm from raw edges, leaving a 31cm gap in stitching at centre. Press seam open and seam allowance to the wrong side along the central opening.

3 Inserting the zip
Refold one seam allowance about 2mm away from original pressed line to form a tiny underlap. Underlap zip tape under

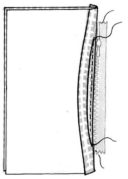

this edge along opening with the zip teeth just next to the fold. Pin, then stitch in place near fold.

4 Finishing the zip
With the right side uppermost, open the back flat. Bring the loose edge of the opening over to just cover the previous row of stitching, and pin to zip tape.

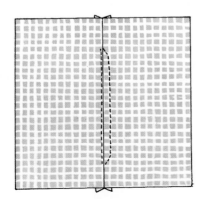

Stitch zip in place 1cm from the fold, shaping stitching at ends as shown.

Always leave the zip half open once mounted; otherwise you will find it difficult to turn the cover right side out when the edge seams are completed.

5 Piping the cover
Join bias strips to make 156cm when all ends are joined to form a circle. Make piping with stitching 1.5cm from raw edges. With raw edges level, pin piping around edge on right side of back, snipping seam allowance to fit around corners. If you have difficulty fitting the piping around the corners, make one snip at the corner, then snip again at each side, 5mm away from first snip. Using a zipper foot, stitch in place along piping stitching line.

6 Joining the cover
With right sides together, stitch front to back around edge with stitching just inside previous row. Trim seam allowance at corners. Turn right side out and press.

Making a frilled cover

Materials
☐ 70cm × 120cm wide fabric
☐ 30cm zip
☐ Matching sewing thread

1 Cutting out
Mark out a 42cm square for front; a piece 42cm × 45cm for back; and two frills each 120cm × 13cm. Cut out. Insert zip in back piece as before.

2 Preparing the frill
With right sides together and taking a narrow seam allowance, stitch short edges of frills to form one circle. Press seams open. With right side outside, press in half lengthways. Seams will be positioned at corners; mark with pins the other two corner points midway between seams.

Stitch gathering thread in two segments with joins midway between corner points where they will be easier to handle. Stitch two rows of gathering stitches through the double thickness of frill, one row 1.5cm from the raw edges

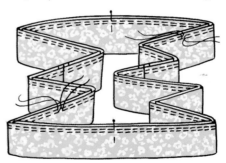

and the other midway between the first and the raw edges.

3 Joining the cover
With raw edges level, place frill around edge of right side of back. Match corner points to corners and pull gathers to fit; arrange more gathers around the corners and a lesser amount along the straight sides. Pin in place and snip into seam allowance of frill at corners to just outside the inner row of gathering.

With right sides together, stitch front to back along previous stitching line.

Trim seam allowance at corners. Turn right side out and press.

Making a flanged cover

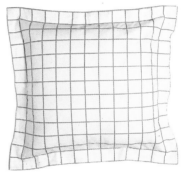

Materials
☐ 50cm × 120cm wide fabric (allow 10cm extra for arranging position of checks if required)
☐ 30cm zip
☐ Matching sewing thread

1 Cutting out
Cut out a 49cm square for front; and a piece 49cm × 52cm for back. Insert zip in the back piece as before.

2 Making the cover
With right sides together, stitch front to back around edge, making the check lines fall exactly on the seamline if using

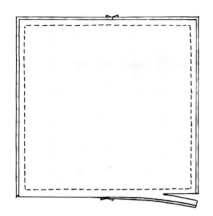

check fabric. Trim corners and seam allowance to about 7mm. Turn right side out and press seam to edge.

3 Making the flange

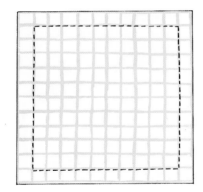

From right side topstitch 3.5cm in from finished edge all round.

Making a contrast fabric cover

Materials

☐ 50cm × 120cm wide main colour fabric
☐ 25cm square contrast fabric for centre inset
☐ 30cm zip
☐ Thread to match main fabric colour

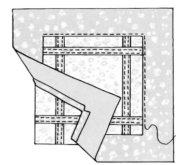

1 Cutting out

From main fabric cut a 42cm square for front; a piece 42cm × 45cm for the back; and a strip 100cm × 2cm for decoration. On front cut out a central hole 19cm square. Cut contrast fabric 25cm square. Insert zip in the back piece as before.

2 Making the cover

Press 5mm over to the wrong side along both long edges of the strip. Cut strip into four equal lengths. Place two strips parallel to two opposite edges of centre inset, with outer edges of strips 4.5cm in from outer edges of inset and raw ends turned under.

Stitch in place along both edges of strips. Stitch other two strips parallel to remaining edges in the same way.

Snip into seam allowances at corners of hole on front. Press 1.5cm seam allowance to wrong side around hole. With raw edges level and right sides uppermost place centre inset behind hole. Pin, then topstitch in place near to folded edge of main piece.

With right sides together stitch front to back around edge. Trim seam allowance at corners. Turn through to right side and press seam to edge.

Patchwork motifs are ideally suited to square cushions. With contrasting colours or a busy pattern, however, a plain, simple cover looks better than one with a frill or flange.

Lacy cushions

These delicate cushions will grace any bedroom or lounge. Made in all white, or another plain colour, they give a subtle and elegant effect. The cushion shapes are very easy to make, and the lace decoration, which looks so rich and elaborate, is in fact very simple to apply.

Before you begin

When selecting your fabrics, bear in mind that crease resistance and washability are useful qualities for cushions that are used regularly. More delicate fabrics or antique lace are best reserved for occasional use and dry cleaned only. Look for shiny or matt surfaces to contrast with each other, and always hold fabrics near to each other to check tones as there are actually many different shades of 'white'.

Choosing lace

Select motifs which either match or complement each other. Try to choose fabrics made of similar fibres: do not mix natural cotton and synthetic lace, for instance, as the colours and textures will vary greatly.

Making cushion covers

Always aim to make your cushion cover slightly smaller than the measurement of the cushion pad at the widest point, up to a maximum of 5cm depending on the size of the pad and the stiffness of the fabric. A slightly tight fit enables the filling to work into the corners, and gives a plump effect.

Fastenings

Fastenings may be either zips, touch-and-close fastening or stud fasteners. Choose a fastener to suit the weight of your cushion cover fabric. With lightweights like satin or lace, use very light nylon zips. When working with frilled or piped outer seams, it is often easiest to insert the zip straight across the back of the cushion case.

Round cushion pads

Ready-made round cushion pads come in various sizes, 30cm, 35cm, 40cm, 46cm and 51cm being the most widely available. Making your own to a specific size

Both allover lace and broderie Anglaise look exquisite decorated with delicate white lace trimming.

is not difficult, but remember to use ticking or feather-proof cambric for a feather filling (0.5kg for a 40cm pad) or foam chips (0.75kg for the same size pad).

Making a round cushion pad

1 Making the covering

Draw a pattern to the size of circle required. Add 1.5cm all round for turnings. Pin the pattern on to a double layer of cambric and cut out two identical circles. Place these, waxed sides together, and stitch round, 1.5cm from raw edges, leaving an opening 20cm wide. Turn through and press.

2 Completing and filling the pad

Take a bag of feathers and if possible

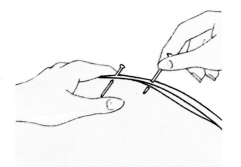

insert the neck of the bag into the opening left in the case. Shake the filling through and hold the gap tightly shut with your fingers until you fold in the edges and pin. Machine stitch round the opening as close as possible to the folded edge. Fasten off ends with back stitches.

Use a lint brush to clean off any spare fluff or down.

Making the broderie Anglaise cushion cover

Materials
For a 35cm square cushion pad
- ☐ 50cm × 90cm white cotton lawn
- ☐ 30cm white broderie Anglaise allover fabric
- ☐ 3m × 8cm wide broderie Anglaise edging
- ☐ 1.50m double-edged broderie Anglaise for ribbon insertion
- ☐ 2.50m white satin ribbon
- ☐ One 35cm white nylon zip

1 Cutting out
Cut out one piece of cotton lawn 39cm square for the front panel and two pieces of cotton lawn 43cm × 24cm for the back.

2 Inserting the zip
Take two back pieces and trim 5mm

17

along one 43cm edge of each piece by either zig-zag stitching or pinking. Press the finished edge over 2cm to wrong side of each piece. Open out the fold on one side and place the zip face down along the

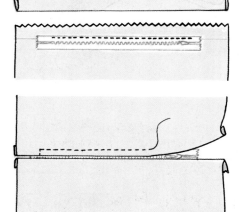

crease line. Centralize the zip and pin along the right side of the teeth. Machine stitch, using a zipper foot. Fold the seam back to the wrong side. From the right side, pin and stitch down the other edge of the zip close to the teeth. The two back pieces are now joined by the zip.

3 Decorating the front

Cut out a square from newspaper 39cm square. Fold in half, and half again, to find the centre. Now unfold, and take in one of the corners to meet the central point. Cut across this fold. Use this triangle to cut four broderie Anglaise pieces, adding 1cm to the diagonal side as shown. Position each triangle of broderie Anglaise right side up on the main fabric cover, taking care to align the corners exactly. Now pin and stitch all edges to

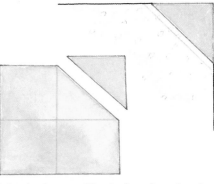

join the layers. Check that the triangles remain flat.

4 Adding the trimming

Cut four lengths of double-edged broderie Anglaise edging 30cm (allowing for a fold at each end to neaten). Pin one side of the trimming to cover the raw edge of the broderie Anglaise, forming a square on

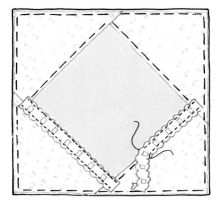

the cushion front. Stitch down both sides of the trimming, overlapping squarely at the corners.

5 Making the frilled edge

Take the 3m × 8cm wide edging for the outer frill and fold to divide into four pieces 75cm long. Mark each fold with a pin or tailor's tack. Make a French seam to join edging into a circle. Run a row of

large machine stitch 1cm down from raw edge and pull the bottom thread to gather up the lace until each quarter measures the same as one side of the finished cover.

6 Attaching the frill

With the right side of the edging down on the right side of the cover, pin the edging so that the seamline will fall 2cm from the outer edge. Match up the pins marking the quarters with the corners of the cushion front. Always allow extra fullness in lace or broderie Anglaise frills

at corners so that they do not pull when the cushion cover is turned right side out. Pin, tack and machine stitch the frill in place.

7 Joining front and back

Place cover pieces right sides together allowing the 2cm surplus of the back piece to extend equally round all sides. Keeping the edging frill well tucked in,

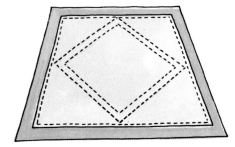

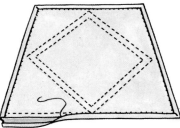

pin, tack and stitch on top of the seamline where the frill was attached. Remember to keep the zip open. Finish the edges by folding the surplus of the back cover over twice to form a narrow binding. Hemstitch to finish on the allowance of the joining seam.

8 Finishing the cushion

Turn the cover through to the right side and push out the corners squarely. Thread narrow ribbon through the broderie Anglaise round the centre square and tie bows at the corners.

Making the triple frill cushion cover

Materials

For a 35cm square cushion pad
☐ 50cm × 90cm white polyester satin
☐ 6.50m × 8cm wide white lace
☐ 1.30m frilled lace with holes for ribbon insertion

□ 2m × 1cm wide white satin ribbon
□ One 35cm white nylon zip

1 Cutting out
Follow the instructions for the broderie Anglaise cushion cover to cut out and make the back cover with zip insertion. Cut out front square as before.

2 Making the front
Use a cool iron to fold and mark lines 2cm, 7cm and 11cm in from the outer edges. Cut three lengths of lace trimming, 3m, 2m and 1.5m. Join and divide into four, then gather as before. The big frill will measure 35cm each quarter, to fit the outer edge, and is attached right side facing down, frill facing inwards, 2cm from the edge of the cover, as for previous cushion. Gather the 2m length to fit 25cm on each side, then pin and topstitch, right side up on top of the cover

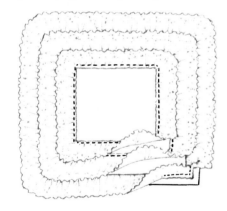

and raw edges to centre. Repeat for the third frill, which measures 17cm for each quarter.

3 Applying the lace trim
Take the narrow lace edging and pin

Scale down the pattern for the broderie Anglaise cushion, or any other cushion, to make this sweet little pot-pourri bag.

round the inside square, over the row of topstitching, pleating the corners just slightly. Machine stitch close to the edges of the trim.

4 Joining front and back covers
Finish the cushion as described for the broderie Anglaise cover. Thread ribbon

through the lace edging all round the centrepiece and tie in a bow to finish.

Making the floral lace cushion cover

Materials
For a 35cm diameter round cushion pad
□ 50cm × 90cm white satin fabric
□ 30cm white allover lace fabric
□ 4m × 5cm wide white lace edging
□ One 35cm white nylon zip

1 Cutting out
Using a 39cm square of paper, cut out a circle template. From this cut a circle of white satin, 39cm diameter, and a second circle by folding the fabric in half, then the pattern in half, and placing it 2.5cm

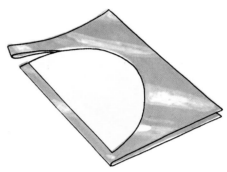

from the fold in the fabric. This allows for mounting the zip into the back cover. For the centre piece, cut a circle of lace fabric, 22cm diameter.

2 Preparing the back
Cut through the centre fold of the back circle. Mount the zip in the centre of the back cover as before.

3 Preparing the front
Fold the smaller satin circle and the lace circle into four to find the centre points:

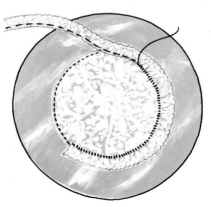

19

match up and pin the lace on top of the right side of the satin. Tack, then straight machine stitch in place close to the edge. Cut a frill 1.5m in length, gather up evenly to fit round the centre piece, a circumference of 70cm. Pin and tack, on top of the cover then topstitch using a close zig-zag stitch, overlapping the ends of the lace and joining and neatening the ends by hand.

4 Making the frill

For the outer frill, cut a length 2.5m long and gather to fit a circumference of 111cm. Place right side facing down on

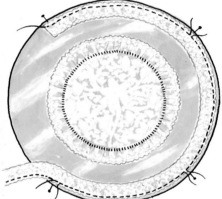

top of the cover, frill towards the centre, and stitch in place 2cm from the outer edge. Overlap the ends and finish by hand as before.

5 Finishing the cover

Join front to back as for the broderie Anglaise cover.

Opposite page and left: Here are some other ideas for romantic lacy cushions, using lace, broderie Anglaise, ribbon, even lace handkerchiefs and tablemats. Choose either white, cream or delicate pastel colours.

Making the cotton lace cushion cover

Materials

For a 35cm diameter round cushion pad
- ☐ 2.50m × 12cm wide cotton lace with both edges finished or 5m × 6cm wide cotton lace with one edge finished
- ☐ 90cm × 6cm wide flat cotton insertion lace
- ☐ 50cm × 90cm white cotton fabric
- ☐ One 35cm white nylon zip
- ☐ 90cm × 15mm wide white satin ribbon

1 Making the back

Cut out and make the back cover as for floral lace cushion.

2 Preparing the front

Cut out the front as for the floral lace

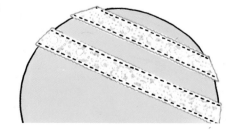

cushion cover. Cut the insertion lace into two pieces, 45cm and 35cm. Place the longer piece diagonally across the right side of the cover, about 18cm from the outer edge. Position the shorter piece about 3cm from the first, and parallel. Pin and topstitch.

3 Attaching the frill

If using the 6cm wide lace, cut it into two equal lengths and with right sides upwards lap one straight edge just over the other, and stitch to form a double-sided lace. Fold the cover and the lace length into quarters, and mark with pins or tailor's tacks. Now pin the lace 2cm from the edge of the cover, section by

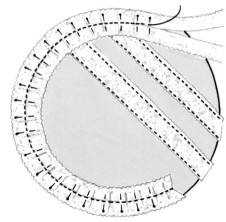

section, making little tucks, on the right side of the cover. Check that the lace is evenly positioned, then zig-zag stitch through the centre of the lace, overlapping the ends and finishing these with hand sewing.

4 Finishing the cover

Join the top and bottom cover pieces as before. Turn the cover through to the right side, and form four small bows with ribbon. Handstitch them to the centre line of the lace edging, inside the frill, at the four quarter points.

CHAPTER 2

And so to bed

The bedroom is one room in which you can really go to town
with soft furnishings, since practical considerations about
wear and tear are not so pressing here.

One of the main considerations when it comes to furnishing a bedroom is the type of bed linen you are going to use. Even before you choose a style and a colour scheme, you will have to decide whether you are going to use a duvet, or sheets, blankets and a bedspread.

Duvets

The duvet has the advantage of being light but warm at the same time. Many people, particularly children, find the ease of bed-making an added attraction.

When buying a duvet, you will have to choose between natural and synthetic fillings—and there are several grades available in each. Generally considered the best (and most expensive) is a pure down filling. Then comes down-and-feather, and next, feather-and-down. The labelling will indicate the filling, and also give a tog rating, which is an indication of the heat insulation properties of the duvet. As well as being natural, and therefore less likely to cause discomfort through perspiration, feathery fillings have the advantage that you can shake down the filling in the summer to reduce insulation.

Synthetic fillings and their tog ratings are also indicated on the label. Some of the newest fibres have been specially developed to reproduce the characteristics of feathers as faithfully as possible. Synthetic fillings are particularly suitable for people who suffer from hay fever, asthma or other allergies, as natural fillings can cause irritation.

Whatever type of duvet you choose, it should be large enough to give a 45cm overhang at the sides and foot of the bed. You should always use a duvet cover,

Lace and ribbon trimmings complement a soft pastel fabric in this duvet cover with matching pillowcases and valance.

either ready-made from one of the many ranges of coloured, patterned and co-ordinated ranges available, or made up from sheeting fabric to co-ordinate with the furnishings in your bedroom.

You will also need a fitted bottom sheet and, if your bed has an unsightly sprung base, you will need a valance. This is a deep frill designed to cover the bed base. Some valances are now incorporated with the bottom sheet, so that a single fitted valanced sheet fits over the mattress and hangs to floor level. Valanced sheets save on the initial outlay, but a separate valance will not wear out so quickly or need washing as often as the bottom sheet.

Blankets and bedspreads

The alternative to the duvet is sheets and blankets. Again, the blankets may be in natural or man-made fibres—from luxurious mohair to acrylic. Man-made blankets will be easier to wash and are often woven with special pockets for extra insulation.

In terms of décor, one of the advantages of blankets is that you can cover them with a bedspread which enhances the style of your room. A neat, tailored bedspread with box pleats at the corners and piping to emphasize the outline of the bed can help turn a bed in a spare room or teenage room into a sofa by day. A fitted cover with a gathered valance adds a romantic touch, while a throwover cover can suit many styles.

While choosing your bed linen, don't forget the pillows. Here too the choice is between natural and man-made fillings. Which you choose will depend on your personal preference for firmer or softer pillows, and your budget.

Colours and fibres

The range of bed linen available is vast—from white broderie Anglaise to black satin. However, most people settle for plain or patterned cotton/polyester, which is easy to wash and needs hardly any ironing. Also, cotton/polyester is reasonably priced and available in an ever increasing range of colours and patterns.

More and more duvet covers are made with some sort of border pattern, designed to fit in with the size and shape of the duvet. And pillows are often available to match, sometimes with a slightly scaled-down design. Such patterns give the bed a sense of importance as the focal point in a bedroom.

Many ranges of bed linen are available through wallcovering manufacturers, and have been specially designed to co-ordinate with wallcoverings and cotton fabrics, to make bedroom colour scheming easy. If you select from these ranges, do try to ensure that the patterns feature differences in scale. If curtains, wallpaper and duvet cover or bedspread are all made from exactly the same pattern, the effect can be either very bland or, at the other extreme, very busy and almost claustrophobic, depending on the scale of the pattern.

There are theories that certain colours are more restful than others; calm blues and greens, or soft pinks and creams are popular bedroom shades. But there is no reason why you shouldn't be a little more adventurous. There are bed linens in splashy, modern prints, bold stripes and bright, primary colours. Such patterns can be stimulating in children's rooms, or liven up an adult bedroom.

A patterned duvet cover in a child's room, with plain carpets, plain walls and painted furniture will brighten up the room, and as the duvet cover is changed over the years, it can alter the character of the room. Fairytale characters, bright bunches of balloons, comic strip heroes, sophisticated stripes—as the duvet wears out, change it to suit your child's tastes.

Adding interest

There are plenty of other ways in which to use fabrics in the bedroom. Attract attention to the bedhead, a focal point in a bedroom, with a padded headboard. Choose fabric for the headboard to match other fabric in the room so you do not have too many competing fabrics. It could match the bedspread, or, with a plain duvet cover, the headboard fabric could be patterned to match curtains. If the duvet cover comes from a co-ordinating range of fabrics and wall-papers, you could use a plain colour for the walls and choose a co-ordinating patterned fabric for the headboard and curtains.

On a grander scale, there are many ways to turn an ordinary bed into a dreamland, with elaborate drapes, canopy or a tester (curtains hung from a plain or carved canopy at the head of the bed). The addition of a wooden framework turns an ordinary bed into a fourposter—but rather than the traditional, draught-excluding curtains, dress it with fine, light fabrics for a more romantic effect: muslin, cotton net, or panels of lace, according to your budget.

There are, of course, many other ways to introduce soft furnishings into the bedroom. Full curtains and a liberal scattering of cushions enhance the soft fabric look. Another nice touch if you have room is to add a small, Victorian-style upholstered chair. The dressing table can also be embellished with fabric—the kidney-shaped dressing table, complete with glass top and curtains, is making a come-back, and even the dullest of dressing tables can be covered with a cloth. A simple circular bedside table can also be dressed up with layers of co-ordinating cloths. And of course lampshades, lined baskets, and other bags and pouches all have their place and their uses in the bedroom.

Top left: Patterned duvet covers can be easily changed to suit children's tastes as they grow older.

Bottom left: With a busy, patterned wallpaper, plain bed linen in a toning colour often looks best.

Above: A patchwork bedspread with co-ordinating curtains and valance looks stunning in shades of one colour.

Quilted bedhead

This quilted cover for a headboard not only gives extra comfort and softness but also adds a decorative feature to a bedroom. The padded and ruched border, edged with piping, completes the cover and adds a touch of elegance.

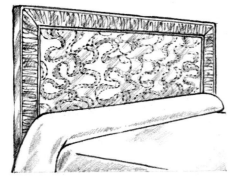

Before you begin
You could make this cover to fit over an existing headboard or construct a simple frame using chipboard. The headboard shown here is made with legs, in which case it is either free-standing and held in position against the wall by the bed frame, or attached to the bed base. It is made to stand 43cm above the floor with the base of the headboard 8cm below the top of the bed.

Quilting
Quilting is often done on a plain fabric with a shiny surface which shows off the design to good effect, contrasting the raised and flat areas. Designs using a straight stitching in geometric designs are popular and easy to achieve for the beginner. However, the design will have to be planned and transferred on to the top fabric. To save time, use a patterned fabric with a simple, clear design and machine or hand stitch round all or part of the outline. This method highlights the printed design and enhances the fabric.

When using the printed pattern on the fabric as the quilting design, the choice of fabric is most important. Look for a simple design with soft curves, otherwise you will have difficulty in manoeuvring the bulk of fabric under the arm of the sewing machine. The outline should not be too small or circular. Quilting is worked through three layers of material: a backing of mull, a top fabric and wadding sandwiched in between. Practise machine quilting on a sample before starting the cover to familiarize yourself with turning the fabric. If you do not feel proficient enough to quilt by machine, it can be done by hand using a running stitch.

Fabric
Choose a fabric with a sheen to show off the quilting to advantage. A printed cotton chintz is ideal in that, as well as having a shiny surface, it is a firm, closely woven fabric. For the border, choose a plain contrasting or toning fabric.

Calculating amounts
For the frame you will need a piece of 2cm thick chipboard the width of the bed by 61cm high. For the legs you will need two pieces of 5cm × 2.5cm softwood batten, each 97cm long, and ten chipboard screws 4cm long.

To calculate the required amount of patterned fabric, first decide on the size of the centre panel and the width of the border. Depending on the width of the centre panel and the width of the chosen fabric, you will need once or twice the height of the centre panel, plus 4cm for hem and seam allowances. You will need to make an allowance over the width and height for a reduction in size during quilting. As a guide, the centre panel for a 137cm wide bedhead was reduced by 10cm across the width and 4cm across the height. The pattern should run from top to bottom of the panel; if you have to join fabric to achieve the required

width, an allowance should be made for matching the pattern.

To estimate the amount of fabric required for the ruched border, multiply the height of the headboard by four, and the width by two; add up the two measurements. You will need sufficient fabric to make a strip this length by the required width of the border, plus 4cm for seam allowances.

For the plain back of the cover, add 2cm to the height and 4cm to the width of the headboard to account for its depth. You will need once or twice the height measurement, including the depth allowance, depending on the width of the bed and the width of the chosen fabric. Remember to add a further 2cm all round for hem and seam allowances.

If two widths of fabric are required to cover the back of the headboard, use the remainder of the second width to cut bias strips to cover the piping cord. If you only need one width (in the case of a single bed), or if you wish to have a contrasting piping, allow an extra 40cm for this purpose.

For the backing to the quilting you will need a length of mull to the width of the headboard, plus a 2cm seam allowance all round, plus an allowance for reduction during quilting.

You will need the same amount of synthetic wadding, plus 40cm to make up the padding for the two sides of the border. The padding for the top of the border can be cut out from alongside the length for the headboard cover.

Finally, you will need enough No. 3 piping cord to go round the centre panel and outer edge of the headboard and 20cm of touch-and-close fastener for tabs at the base of the cover.

A printed fabric with a distinct design lends itself well to quilting.

Materials
For a cover to fit a headboard which is 137cm wide

☐ 60cm × 140cm wide printed chintz
☐ 2.10m × 130cm wide plain chintz
☐ 1.60m × 90cm wide mull
☐ 1.90m × 98cm wide heavyweight wadding
☐ 5m of No. 3 piping cord
☐ 20cm touch-and-close fastener
☐ Matching sewing thread

For the frame

☐ A piece of chipboard, 137cm × 61cm × 2cm
☐ Two softwood battens, 5cm × 2.5cm × 97cm
☐ Ten 4cm long chipboard screws
☐ Four 7.5cm long screws are required if the frame is to be attached to the base of the bed.

Making-up instructions

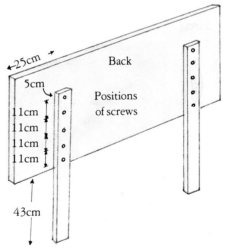

1 Making the frame

Lay the chipboard on the floor and draw a line parallel to each short side 25cm in from edges. Mark a line on each batten 43cm from one end. Mark the positions of the screws on the battens. Drill holes in the battens for the screws, allowing for countersinking the heads (the heads finish flush with the batten).

27

Place the drilled battens on the chipboard aligning the outer side of the batten with marked line on chipboard and positioning the bottom mark on battens level with the bottom edge of the chipboard panel. Push a bradawl through the drill holes of the batten into the chipboard to form starter holes for the screws. Insert screws into holes to secure the battens to the chipboard.

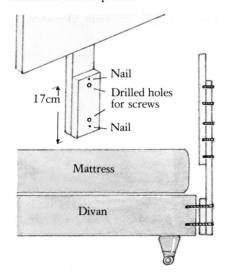

If you are attaching the bedhead to the bed base, cut off the bottom 17cm from each batten. Nail the sawn off section to each shortened leg. Drill two holes into each shortened leg (plus blocks) for screws. Place bedhead in position and insert large 7.5cm screws into the base of the bed.

2 Preparing for quilting

Cut out one piece of mull 151cm× 70cm, one piece of wadding 147cm× 66cm, and one piece of top fabric for the centre panel 127cm×58cm. Press the fabric before you start to quilt, as you cannot press it afterwards.

Lay the mull out flat. Place wadding on top, leaving a 2cm seam allowance of mull showing all round. Tack the wadding to the mull quite close to the edge.

Centre fabric for quilting, right side uppermost, on top, with bottom raw edge level with raw edge of mull. Tack all three thicknesses together with a contrasting thread vertically and horizontally through the centre. Continue to tack further rows on each side of the central tacking lines, approximately 7.5cm apart, until the whole area has been covered. This is an important part of the quilting process. The three layers must be held firmly together or they will slip and pucker during the quilting. Mark the seamline round the centre panel, 2cm in from the raw edge, with tacking in a contrasting colour.

3 Quilting

Roll up excess fabric that you are not working on in order to manoeuvre it under the arm of the machine. Machine stitch, following the outline of your chosen design and smooth out the fabric on each section you are working on to avoid puckering where lines cross. Do not stitch over the seamline of the centre panel. If your machine has a speed control, place it on minimum speed for more control. If you find this process difficult, quilt the design by hand using a running stitch. When the quilting is completed, remove all the tacking. Measure panel to check size.

4 Piping

Cut enough 5cm wide bias strips to fit round the centre panel and outer edge of

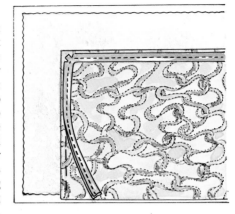

the headboard and cover the piping cord following the instructions on pages 10–11. Pin and tack the covered piping cord to the seamline around the centre panel with the raw edges level. Clip into

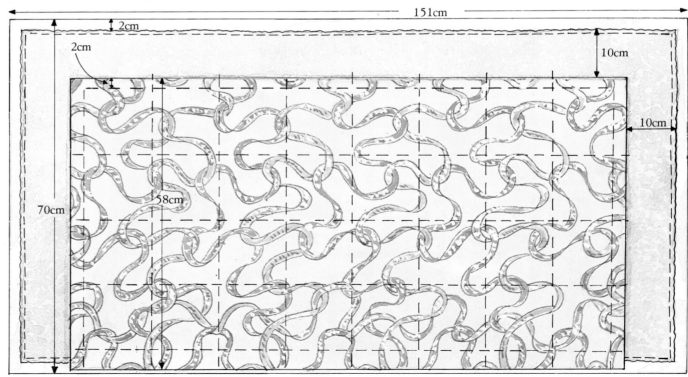

the seam allowances of the piping at corners to ease. Machine stitch in place using a zipper foot.

5 Preparing the ruched border

Cut four widths of fabric, each 17cm wide. With right sides together, join two strips together across the short ends, taking a 2cm seam allowance. These two lengths will gather up to form the top border. With right sides together, join another strip to each end of the top border, mitring the corners, to form side borders. To form the mitre, fold the fabric, right sides together and raw edges level, pin and stitch diagonally across the border from the outer edge to the inside edge. Machine a row of gathering stitches (long stitches, loose tension) 2cm away from the raw edge on both sides of the border. Machine a second row of

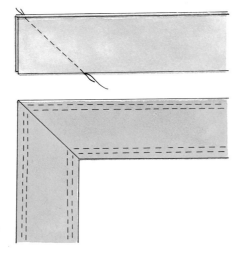

stitching 5mm away from the first within the seam allowance.

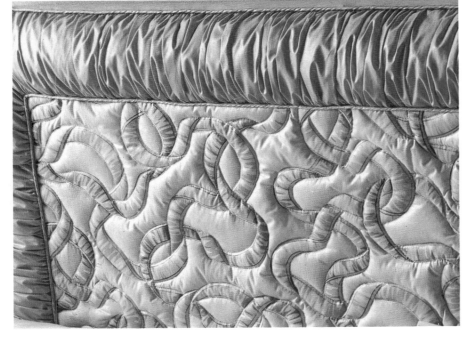

Chintz fabric has enough sheen to show off quilting to advantage.

6 Finishing the inner edge

Placing right sides together and pulling up the gathering threads, pin and tack the inner edge of the border to the seamline of the quilted panel, spacing gathers evenly and positioning the mitred corners of the border at the corners of the quilted panel. Machine stitch in place using a zipper foot.

7 Padding the border

From the remaining wadding, cut a strip the width of the centre panel by 20cm wide for the top roll, and two strips the height of the headboard by 20cm for the side rolls. Fold each strip in half lengthways and oversew the cut edges together to form three rolls. Having removed tacking holding the mull and wadding together round the outer edge, place the appropriate padding roll in position between the mull and wadding along the border. Sew ends of top roll to the side rolls. Replace the wadding border over the rolls and restitch the wadding to the mull on the seamline, enclosing the padding rolls.

8 Finishing the outer edge

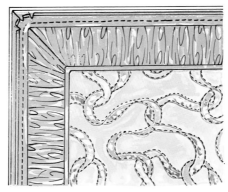

Gather up the outer edge of the ruched border to fit the outer edge of the padded border. Space gathers evenly. Tack the

ruched border to the seamline of the mull enclosing the wadding. Pin and tack the piping over this seamline with raw edges level. Clip seam allowances of piping at corners to ease round. Stitch in place using the zipper foot.

9 Completing the back

Cut one width of plain fabric, 70cm long. Cut two strips 70cm × 9.5cm. Join a strip to each side of the full width of fabric, taking a 2cm seam allowance.

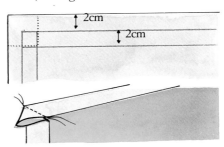

Stitch and press seams open. On the wrong side, mark the seamline all round 2cm in from the raw edge with chalk. Mark a second line 2cm in from the seamline down the sides and along the top. This line will lie at the back edge of the headboard. With right sides together, join top edge to side edge for 4cm to form a corner to fit over the back of the headboard.

With right sides together, pin and tack the back of the cover to the front along the seamline, sandwiching the piping on the outer edge of the ruched border in between. Machine stitch using a zipper foot. Change zipper foot to a general purpose foot and zig-zag stitch the seam allowances close to the original stitching. Trim close to the stitching.

Turn up a 1cm wide double hem along the bottom edges and stitch, attaching 5cm long strips of touch-and-close fastener 20cm and 50cm from each side edge along both hems.

Monogrammed bed linen

Bed linen made entirely in white, with lace insertion and delicately embroidered monograms, looks exquisite and makes a refreshing change from the ubiquitous duvet cover. It is ideal for a wedding present and relatively inexpensive too.

Before you begin

Making your own sheets is very easy even for the beginner. Most stores sell cotton/polyester sheeting up to 228cm wide, which is easy to care for and needs little or no ironing. White or pale pastels look best, with the monogram embroidered in the same colour. A simple lace insertion further enhances the beauty of the bed linen. Cotton lace is best, although nylon lace can also be used provided it is not too flimsy. If using cotton lace, wash it before use, as it will shrink. Before buying the required

Use pastel fabrics and embroidery thread for monogrammed linen.

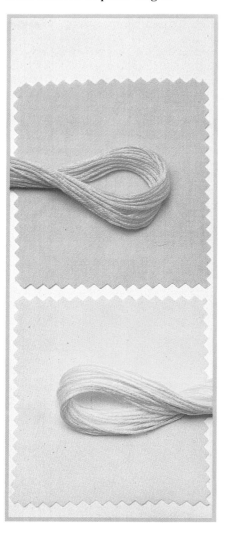

length, test wash a 10cm piece of the selected lace and measure how much it shrinks. If it shrinks 1cm, buy 10% more than the required length.

Calculating the amounts

To work out the required width of sheeting, measure the width of the mattress including the depth; add a 30cm tuck-in allowance for a double bed and 25cm for a single bed. Round up to the nearest width of sheeting and use the entire width so as to avoid side hems.

To estimate the required length of sheeting, measure length of mattress including the depth. Add 25cm−30cm for hems and tuck-in.

For the pillow cases, measure the length and width of the pillow and add 2cm all round for seam allowances. You will need two pieces this size for each pillow, plus one piece the width measurement (including seam allowances) by 20cm.

The lace needs to be 4cm longer than the finished width of the sheet or pillow case, plus an allowance for shrinkage.

Making the sheet

Materials

For a top sheet for a standard double bed
- ☐ 2.90m × 228cm wide cotton/ polyester sheeting
- ☐ 10cm × 7cm lightweight iron-on interfacing
- ☐ 1 skein Anchor stranded embroidery cotton in white, 0402

- ☐ 2.50m × 6cm wide white cotton lace
- ☐ No. 8 crewel needle
- ☐ 15cm embroidery hoop

1 Preparing the fabric for the embroidery

Cut out the required length of sheeting. Fold it in half lengthways to find the

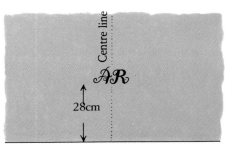

centre; mark by finger pressing along the fold for about 30cm from one end. From the same end, measure 28.5cm and mark a short line at right angles to the fold line. This will mark the base of the monogram. Transfer the required letters on to the fabric, taking care to position them the right way up. Pin a piece of iron-on interfacing to the back of the fabric underneath the letters and tack in place. Stretch the fabric in an embroidery hoop before beginning to embroider.

2 Embroidering the letters

Using three strands of embroidery cot-

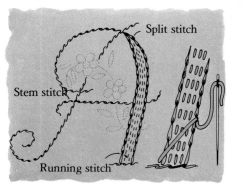

ton, work stem stitch along the single lines of the letters and split stitch on the double lines. Make two rows of running stitch between the rows of split stitch.

Make the first satin stitch at a 45° angle across the widest part of the letter and work all subsequent stitches first to one side and then to the other. On curved areas the satin stitches may be closer together on one side than on the other so as to fit into the curve.

3 Finishing the monogram
Work the flower stems in stem stitch and outline the leaves and flowers in split stitch. Fill in the leaves with satin stitch

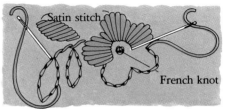

worked diagonally. To fill in the flowers, work satin stitch from the edge inwards, and finish the centre with a French knot.

4 Removing interfacing
Remove the fabric from the embroidery hoop and carefully cut away the excess

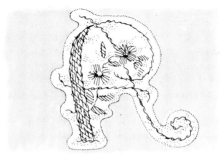

interfacing. Place right side down over a pad and press.

5 Inserting the lace

Cut a length of lace and place it on the right side of the sheet 1.5cm below the base line of the monogram; pin and tack in place. Stitch by machine as close to the edge as possible along each side. Trim the fabric at the back of the lace to 1cm from each stitching line. Turn under the raw edges nearest monogram; pin, tack and

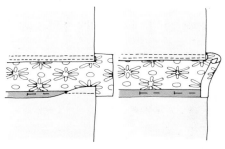

machine stitch. Fold the other trimmed edge away from the lace; press fold. Turn under each raw edge of the lace 1cm and then 1cm again; pin and tack.

6 Finishing the top edge

Turn under the raw edge 1cm then fold 10cm to the wrong side. Pin and tack along the lower edge of lace insertion.

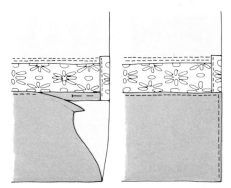

Machine stitch the hem; finish the side edge by stitching from the top edge to the lower edge of the lace.

7 Making the bottom hem

Make a hem at the other end of the sheet by turning under 1cm and then 2cm.

Tack and then stitch in place.
Press all hems.

Making the pillow cases
Materials

For a pair of pillow cases, 50cm × 75cm
- ☐ 1.10m × 229cm wide cotton/ polyester sheeting
- ☐ 1.70m × 6cm wide white cotton lace
- ☐ Two pieces of iron-on interfacing, 10cm × 7cm
- ☐ 1 skein Anchor stranded embroidery cotton in white, 0402
- ☐ No. 8 crewel needle
- ☐ 15cm embroidery hoop

1 Cutting out

To make two pillow cases, you will need two pieces 79cm × 54cm for the backs, two pieces 24cm × 54cm for the tuck-ins and two pieces 79cm × 59cm for the fronts.

The extra 5cm of fabric are necessary in order to fit the fabric in an embroidery hoop.

The excess fabric is actually trimmed away when the embroidered monogram has been completed.

2 Preparing the front piece

Mark the vertical centre line and measure 13.5cm down this line from the raw edge; mark a short line across and at right angles to the centre line. Use this line as the base line when transferring the

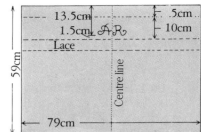

monogram. Embroider the monogram in the same way as for the sheet; trim away excess 5cm above the embroidery. Cut the lace to exactly the same length as the front piece and insert as for the sheet, 1.5cm below the monogram. Trim fabric and neaten raw edges as for the edge nearest the monogram on the sheet.

3 Joining the pieces

Make a 1cm wide double hem along one short side of the back and down the long side of the tuck-in. Join the back and the tuck-in to the front with French seams. Begin and end each stitching line 1cm from the raw edge.

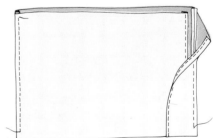

Fold the back over the front, right sides together, and fold the tuck-in over the back. Join top and bottom edges with bound seams: stitch across the pillow case 2cm from the raw edges. Trim one seam allowance, fold the wider seam allowance over the narrower one and stitch again. Turn right side out.

Appliquéd story quilt

This charming cot quilt, with Goldilocks and the three bears in appliqué, will keep your baby comfortable while fast asleep.

It is simple to make, very economical and fully washable.

Before you begin

The design for this quilt has been taken from the story of Goldilocks and the three bears, but any fairy-tale or nursery rhyme could provide characters and motifs for an interesting quilt. From an illustrated book, you could easily trace the motifs, divide each picture into squares and enlarge it as required, using dressmaker's graph paper.

Fabrics and filling

A cot quilt requires frequent washing, and all materials should therefore be pre-shrunk and colourfast. A cotton/polyester poplin is suitable for the back and front; use synthetic wadding for the filling. The appliqué motifs can be made from leftover scraps of plain and printed cottons and cotton mixtures. If you use 100% cotton, wash the fabrics first to prevent shrinkage later. Try to choose an appropriate fabric for each motif. For example, on this quilt Goldilocks' apron is made from broderie Anglaise, the tablecloth from gingham, the flower borders from floral prints, and so on. The border fabric has a stripe in a contrasting colour, which acts as a guide for the quilting.

Calculating amounts

Decide on desired size of the finished quilt. You will need two pieces each of poplin and medium-weight wadding the same size as the finished quilt, plus 1.5cm all round for seam allowances. Scraps of assorted fabrics are sufficient for the appliqué.

Materials

For a quilt measuring 75cm × 110cm
- ☐ 1.60m × 115cm wide cream poplin
- ☐ 60cm × 115cm wide printed cotton for the border
- ☐ Assorted printed cottons for appliqué motifs
- ☐ Matching sewing threads
- ☐ Iron-on interfacing
- ☐ One small pot each of black, red and blue fabric paint
- ☐ 2.30m × 90cm wide medium-weight wadding
- ☐ Dressmaker's graph paper
- ☐ Fine paint brush

Making-up instructions

1 Cutting out the main pieces
Cut out two poplin pieces, each measuring 113cm × 78cm. Cut two pieces of wadding to the same size. Cut out four 14cm wide border strips, two 113cm long and two 78cm long.

2 Preparing the appliqué motifs
Using dressmaker's graph paper, enlarge all appliqué motifs on the graph to the correct size and cut out the pattern pieces. Back the fabrics selected for the appliqué design with iron-on interfacing. Using the pattern pieces, cut out the motifs from appropriate fabrics. Also cut out several pieces from floral fabric.

3 Painting the features
Using a fine brush and diluting the paint as required, paint the face and hands of Goldilocks and the faces and paws of the three bears. (It is better to do any painting at this stage than when the motifs are already appliquéd, as any mistakes can be discarded.)

4 Making the border
Turn under one long edge on each strip 1cm and place the long strips along the long edges of one poplin piece, raw edges matching; pin in place. Position the short

Use small prints in green for tree foliage, brown for tree trunks, gingham for the tablecloth and floral prints for flower borders. Use small prints or stripes for clothes and broderie Anglaise for the apron.

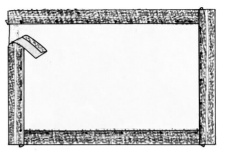

strips along the short edges in the same way and pin in place.

5 Arranging the appliqué

Place all appliqué motifs on the right side of the poplin and move them about until the right balance is achieved. If any pieces overlap the border, tuck them underneath the borders except the trees which

should overlap the border. Pin and tack in place. With a fairly wide, close zig-zag, stitch all the motifs in place, using matching threads. Stitch the border in place all round the inside edge.

6 Quilting the picture

Lay the picture, right side up, on a piece of wadding. Tack all the layers together vertically and horizontally, starting from the centre and working outwards. Quilt

35

by hand with a small running stitch around some of the images.

7 Joining back and front

Place the remaining pieces of wadding and poplin together and tack together as before. Place the front and back together, poplin sides together and raw edges matching. Pin, tack and stitch 1.5cm from the edge all round, leaving a 30cm gap along one short edge. Turn right side out and slipstitch the opening to close.

8 Finishing the quilt

Stitch by machine along the inside and the centre of the border to give a more quilted effect.

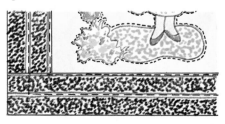

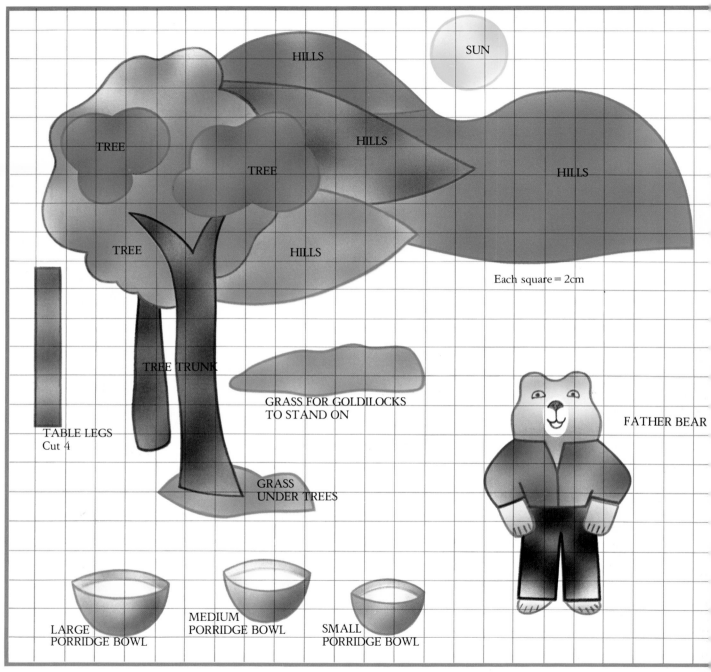

SUN

HILLS

TREE

TREE

HILLS

HILLS

TREE

HILLS

Each square = 2cm

TREE TRUNK

GRASS FOR GOLDILOCKS
TO STAND ON

TABLE LEGS
Cut 4

FATHER BEAR

GRASS
UNDER TREES

LARGE
PORRIDGE BOWL

MEDIUM
PORRIDGE BOWL

SMALL
PORRIDGE BOWL

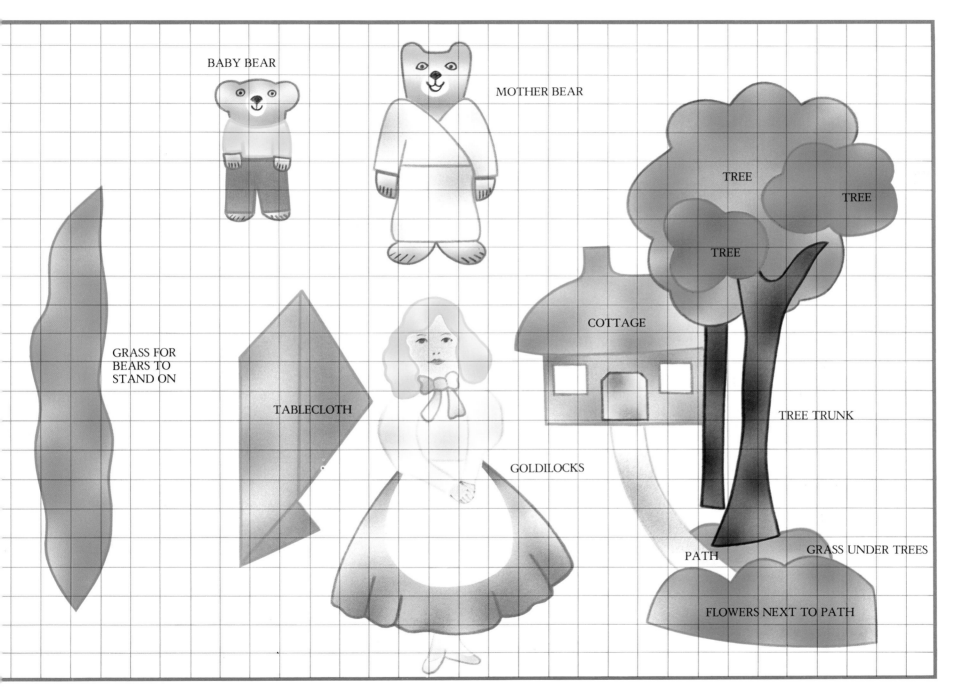

BABY BEAR

MOTHER BEAR

TREE

TREE

TREE

GRASS FOR
BEARS TO
STAND ON

COTTAGE

TABLECLOTH

GOLDILOCKS

TREE TRUNK

PATH

GRASS UNDER TREES

FLOWERS NEXT TO PATH

Patchwork bed cover

The lovely old patchwork quilts we admire in museums, and the modern ones to be seen in craft shops, are usually made entirely by hand. If so, they have involved hours and hours of patient stitching to join together the tiny scraps of brightly coloured materials that make this craft so very attractive.

Not everyone has the time or patience for such painstaking work, but it is possible to reproduce the traditional patterns far more quickly by using a sewing machine to join the pieces together in strips, which are then machined together to make quilts, curtains, dresses or whatever you wish. The patches can, of course, be sewn together by hand if you prefer, or you can use a combination of hand and machine stitching.

With the wealth of beautiful fabrics available in the shops, a modern patchwork quilt can deservedly take its place among the family heirlooms.

Six different fabrics are used for this patchwork quilt, which has a design of plain and patterned squares and triangles and a centre panel with an appliqué motif. This panel is hand-quilted, as are the bands of patchwork.

Before you begin

The choice of fabrics is very important in all patchwork and even more so on something as large as a bed cover. It is important to remember that all fabrics must be of the same weight, pre-shrunk and colourfast, so always test wash a

Use a mixture of light and dark fabrics, some plain and some with small prints.

small piece of the fabric before using it for patchwork.

The colours used must not be too close in tone or the design will not show up clearly. For example, a design in a lot of neutral shades would hardly look like patchwork at all because the colours would simply merge into each other, so choose a mixture of light and dark shades. The areas that will stand out most clearly from a distance will be the very light and the very dark.

Try out the design with fabric samples before buying large quantities, drawing it on to graph paper and colouring with crayons to represent each fabric. By repeating this two or three times and moving the fabrics around, it is possible to assess the different effects of using more or less of one particular fabric.

Calculating amounts of material

This quilt measures 254cm × 236cm, so will fit a large double bed and give

plenty of overhang. You can alter the measurements either by making all the patches a different size or by omitting one or more of the borders. Work out the amount of fabric needed for a different-sized quilt on graph paper. Draw the design on the graph paper, and, allowing 5mm all round for seam allowances, work out how much fabric is required for each path. Multiply this measurement by the number of patches required.

Materials

For a bed cover 254cm × 236cm (the amounts given below are for 122cm wide fabric)
- ☐ 2.20m fabric A (plain cream)
- ☐ 1m fabric B (plain peach)
- ☐ 2m fabric C (peach print)
- ☐ 2.50m fabric D (pale green)
- ☐ 1m fabric E (dark green)
- ☐ 1m fabric F (rust print)
- ☐ 5.10m of backing fabric (or use a large sheet)
- ☐ 7.10m × 90cm of medium-weight polyester wadding
- ☐ Matching thread
- ☐ Thin card for patchwork templates (use old cereal packets)
- ☐ 10m bias binding

Making-up instructions

Each square = 3cm

1 Making the pattern

Using dressmaker's graph paper, draw the appliqué design to the correct scale and cut out the pattern.

Trace the patch templates on to thin cardboard. Make two or three of each size as they become inaccurate very quickly after a few cuttings out.

2 Cutting out the fabric

To cut out the patches, place the template on the wrong side of the fabric. Ensure that all patches are cut on the straight grain. Draw round the template with a fine, sharp pencil or a chalk pencil, which can be frequently sharpened. Remove the template and put it down again 1cm away from the pencil line. Draw round it again in pencil, remove the template and continue like this, always leaving a 1cm space between each pencilled shape.

When cutting out these pencilled patches, cut through the centre of the 1cm spaces with very sharp scissors and this will give a 5mm seam allowance to each patch.

From fabric A, cut out the centre piece

And so to bed

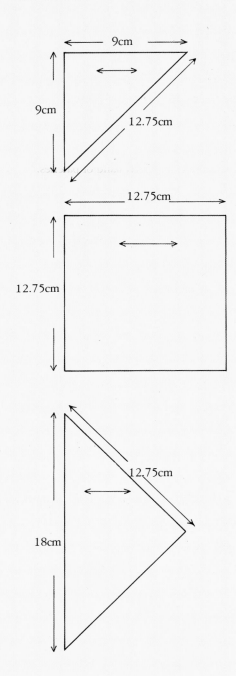

9cm

9cm

12.75cm

12.75cm

12.75cm

12.75cm

18cm

12.75cm

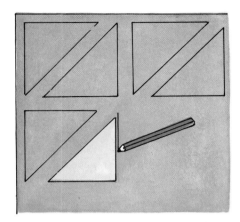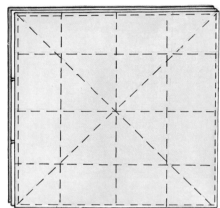

91cm × 73cm, 12 squares, 36 large triangles and 204 small triangles.

From fabric B, cut out 108 small triangles. From fabric C, cut out two strips 163cm × 10cm, two strips 199cm × 10cm and 78 small triangles.

From fabric D, cut out two strips 145cm × 10cm, two strips 109cm × 10cm, two strips 217cm × 10cm, two strips 253cm × 10cm and 30 small triangles.

From fabric E, cut 180 small triangles. From fabric F, cut 96 small triangles.

3 Working the appliqué centre

Using the pattern and leftover fabric, cut out the appliqué shapes. Arrange these as a design in the centre of the oblong. Tack fairly close to the raw edges and press before machining.

Set machine on zig-zag stitch fairly close and quite wide and stitch all round each appliqué motif.

4 Making patchwork borders

Following the colour sequence and taking a 5mm wide seam allowance, join all patches, wrong sides together and raw edges matching, to make squares, then join the squares to make strips. Press all seams open as you go along.

Starting from the centre, join the ap-pliquéd oblong and all subsequent strips, taking a 5mm wide seam allowance. Press all seams open.

5 Backing the quilt

Cut out the backing fabric and the wadding to the same size as the quilt top. On

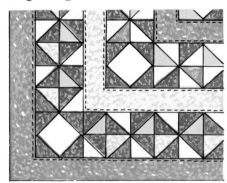

a smooth, flat surface lay the patching wrong side up, place the wadding on top of that and finally the backing, right side up. Keep all the fabrics as smooth and flat as possible. Tack the three layers together in a grid formation, and also diagonally.

6 Quilting

This form of quick quilting simply holds the three layers together, though more elaborate and decorative quilting could equally well be worked on this quilt.

Lay the quilt out on a flat surface. Starting on the appliqué area, pin well all round the design to stop the fabric moving. Using matching thread, work a small running stitch close to the design edge through all three thicknesses. Do the same round each band of patches.

7 Finishing the quilt

Finish off the raw edges of the quilt with bias binding or make bias strips out of leftover fabric and bind the edges with that to finish.

Any number of patchwork designs can be stitched by machine, so long as you use squares, rectangles and triangles rather than diamonds or hexagons.

CHAPTER 3

All lit up

Lampshade making used to require specialized skills. But the popularization of simpler, softer shapes for shades means that even the least skilled needlewoman can try her hand.

he most specialized equipment you will need for lampshade making is a frame. These are made of wire, which is often coated with plastic or painted.

Taping the frame

With most styles of lampshade cover, the first step is to tape the frame. This involves binding the frame tightly with cheap, loosely woven white tape, stitching the ends securely so that the tape will not unravel. With Tiffany-style frames, where the tape will show, you can dye the tape to match before attaching it to the frame.

This tape forms the basis for attaching the lampshade fabric to the frame. As the fabric is stretched in place it can be pinned and then stitched (with close, hand stitches) to the tape-covered frame.

The only other items you need are plenty of pins, some fine needles, and a thimble to help if you like to use one. In some cases the needle will have to be forced through layers of fabric, so a thimble is recommended, even if you don't normally use one.

Suiting the décor

The two real choices for materials for lampshades to make yourself are paper and fabric. Which you choose depends on the effect you are after.

Choose the fabric or paper according to the style of the shade and other fabrics in the room. If you have fabric left over after making curtains or cushions, this is ideal for using to make a soft fabric shade. Wallpaper left from decorating a room is another alternative, but it is not always the best choice, as the lampshade may 'disappear' against the wall pattern.

Traditional lampshades like this one are made panel by panel and bound with crossways strips of self fabric.

Fabric is stretched tightly over the frame for Tiffany-style lampshades.

Where possible, choose plain finishes if they are to be against a patterned surface. Against a plain surface you have the choice of a contrasting or toning colour, or a pattern. If you prefer a pattern, either choose one you have used elsewhere in the room, or select the colours and design very carefully so that patterns do not compete with each other.

If your colour schemes co-ordinate through different rooms in your home, you can happily introduce into one room the wallcovering you have used in an adjacent room—for instance, a hall wallpaper for a living room lampshade, or a bathroom wallcovering for a bedroom shade. (Note: never use free-standing lighting in a bathroom. All bathroom lighting must be specifically designed to meet the required safety standards.)

Choice of fabrics

A furnishing cotton, or better still a finer cotton, is suitable for a soft, pleated fabric lampshade, with a light cotton lining. In a formal setting you may prefer a slub-weave, silky fabric, which looks good lined with a fine lining fabric.

Choose fabrics which do not fray, as they will be easier to work with. And go for tightly woven fabrics, particularly if they have to be stretched tightly over the frame to achieve the look you are after.

Fabric-covered card

If you want to use a fabric which is not suitable, adjust your design and make a card shade, then use the fabric to cover the card, sticking it smoothly in place before you cut the card. With this sort of shade you will not need to tape the frame in the usual way before you start, as the card can be glued in place to special self-adhesive cotton tape stuck to the frame.

Light qualities

When choosing fabric or paper for a lampshade, always make a careful check on the effect when light shines through it. Fabrics may change colour totally, and different types of paper will let varying amounts of light through. Wallpaper, when pleated, will diffuse the light gently; mounted on thicker card, it can be used to make a conical or drum-shaped shade which is very dense.

Plan your lighting with your own specific needs in mind. Generally, a central pendant is most effective fitted with a shade which diffuses the light evenly—like a Japanese paper lampshade. At other times, for example in a dining room, what is needed is a low-hung, fringed lampshade with a pale lining and darker outer fabric reflecting light down on to a table. In a kitchen, a conical card shade can fulfil the same function.

Occasional lighting, too, must be shaded to meet your requirements. A dense, card drum shade makes a pleasing shape on a stout standard lamp. A pale lining will reflect light up and down, but there will be no glare at eye level. A standard lamp placed behind a chair casts a good light for reading or sewing. Lamps set on tables lower in the room must also be well shaded to prevent glare at eye level when you are sitting down. And a shade on a lamp opposite a television must be sufficiently dense to produce a minimum of reflection on the screen.

If you have a fair number of dense shades like these, it's a good idea to keep the ceiling white so that the light that spills upwards from the shade is reflected back down into the room.

One advantage of the simpler, home-made lampshades is that no special light bulbs (or lamps, as they should be called) are required. Pearl 60-watt lamps are probably sufficient in most occasional light fittings, and 100-watt bulbs in central and standard lamps.

Do remember that lampshade frames are designed to be used in a particular way, with fabric stretched well away from the light bulb. Do not try to adapt designs without being sure that they will be safe: even a 60-watt bulb can burn fabric if it is hung too close to it.

Aspects of style

Choose your lampshade not only for the light it casts but also for its style. In a formal setting, with traditional prints and rich textures, a gently shaped shade looks very elegant. If you like an ornate style, there are waisted and tapered shades, circular, rectangular or hexagonal.

Trimmings can also be chosen to fit in with the style—from delicate velvet or satin ribbons to heavy pompons and deep fringing. This is another advantage of making your own lampshades, because the selection of trimmings you can choose from is much greater than on ready-made lampshades.

Quick cover-ups

If you've only a small budget, here are a couple of ideas for dressing up a lamp using less than a metre of fabric.

Take a piece of fabric about 0.75 metre square and neaten the edges with a closed-up zig-zag stitch. Make a hole in the centre and neaten the raw edges. Spray the fabric with a flame retardant. Thread the square on to the flex of a central pendant (after turning off the power) and drape it over a conical lampshade. Ensure that the bulb is of low wattage and does not overheat the fabric.

If you have an unattractive lamp base, make a drawstring bag (with a hole in one corner for the flex if necessary). Slip the bag over the base, thread a ribbon through the top, and tie it at the neck of the lamp to hide the base.

Pleated fabric lampshade

Pleated lampshades are both easy to make and fashionable, calling for less perfect fitting than other lampshade shapes. The fullness of the fabric makes an attractive soft focus for a lighting arrangement, and the folds in the fabric give a pleasant texture.

Before you begin

Cylindrical or conical frames are suitable for this treatment, and even very slightly waisted frames can be used although straight struts are preferable. For the beginner, a cylinder frame is easier to work with, as the pleats around the top and bottom are identical; when working with a conical frame, the bottom pleats need to be fanned out in order to cover the wider ring.

Good colours for lampshades are pinks and yellows because they cast a warm light; choose small designs that work well in pleats.

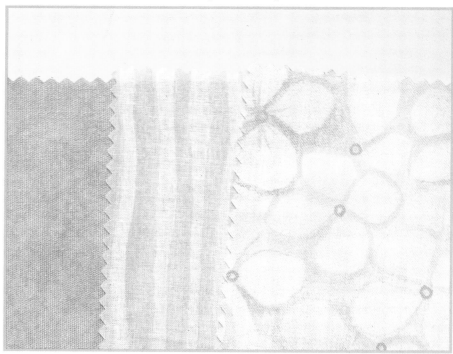

Plastic-coated frames need only be taped around the top and bottom rings, not around the struts. However, if you buy a plain metal, copper-coloured frame, then taping the struts as well is to be recommended, partly because the metal is unattractive, and partly because it may rust and spoil your work if the struts are left untaped.

Suitable fabrics

The main difference in making a pleated lampshade from making a fitted one is that the lining is mounted inside the frame; the cover fabric, as usual, is mounted on the outside of the struts. For a small table light, such as a coolie where the struts are not visible, it is not absolutely necessary to line the shade, as the pleats in the fabric give enough density to dull the light source.

It is important to choose a closely woven fabric—for the lining as well as for the main cover—that will not pull away from the stitching on the top and bottom rings. (For instance, avoid cheap taffeta for the lining.) For the cover, cottons, linens and satins are all good choices as the pleats give bulk; you can choose cheaper dress-weight fabrics if desired. The cut edges are trimmed with self-made bias binding. Bear this in mind when selecting fabric, so that you choose a medium or light weight, not something too thick to be pleated up or to make the bias binding.

As the pleats fan out, choose a fabric with a small irregular pattern that will not be distorted by the pleating.

The lining

As for other lampshades, choose a colour for the lining that will warm up the light source. Peaches, pinks and pale yellows are the best choices, as blues and greens cast a cold light. With a pleated shade, you can have the best of both worlds by choosing a fabric in a blue or soft green if that is the room décor, and line it in a contrasting, warmer colour. The fabric harmonizes with the room when the lamp is unlit, and the lining will create a warm patch of light without detracting from the shade when the lamp is actually switched on.

Calculating amounts

The amount of material required will depend to some extent on the width of pleats you prefer, and whether you decide to space them out or set them close together. The most standard method is to make regular pleats just touching at the top and fan them out at the bottom of the shade. For this method, measure the circumference of the top ring and multiply by three to get the total width of fabric required. The length required will simply be a few centimetres more than the height of the shade to allow for ease of working. Remember to allow extra fabric if you choose a pattern that has a

With conical-shaped lampshades the pleats are fanned out at the bottom.

pronounced repeat, as this should run level all round the shade.

The lining is also pleated, but there is no need to do this as elaborately or carefully as the cover. Roughly 1½ times to twice the circumference of the top ring is ample. The length should be the same as for the main fabric.

For taping the frame allow twice the relevant measurements, plus a little more for safety: the amount used varies from person to person depending on their winding technique.

Materials
For a lampshade 40cm in diameter × 44cm deep
□ 2m × 122cm wide main fabric
□ 1m × 115cm wide lining fabric
□ 5.50m tape for the frame rings
□ Matching sewing thread
□ Fabric adhesive

Making-up instructions

1 Taping the frame
Following the instructions given in step 1 on page 50, tape the upper and lower rings only if the frame is plastic-coated; the struts will be covered by the lining.

2 Mounting the lining
Cut the lining widthways into two equal halves. Starting at one of the struts, fold the selvedge of the lining 2cm to the wrong side and pin the fabric to the top ring with the right side facing into the centre of the frame. Work around the frame on the top ring, forming little pleats, about 1cm deep, and about 4cm apart. Always place the pins at right angles to the struts—facing inwards—to avoid scratching your hands when sewing.

When the top row is pinned, distribute the pleats evenly around the bottom ring, fanning them out slightly if the frame is

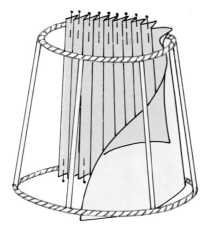

conical. When you have to make a join in the pleating, simply leave the end piece pinned flat, fold 2cm to the wrong side on the new piece and place it over the end of the previous piece, making a pleat and hiding the selvedge at the same time.

3 Stitching the lining
Using a double length of matching thread, oversew through the fabric and tape around the top ring along pinned line, removing the pins as you go. Stitch the bottom ring in the same way, keeping the fabric taut. Keep the stitches as close to the edge of the rings, on the inside, as

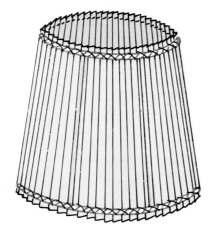

possible. When completed, trim off all surplus lining fabric, top and bottom, cutting very close to the frame without breaking the stitches.

4 Mounting the cover fabric
Cut the fabric into four lengths, 50cm long. You will use up three whole

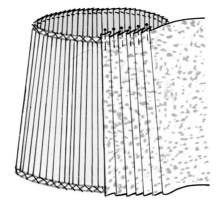

widths, plus part of the fourth width, leaving a piece which will be used for the bias binding. Trim off the white selvedges. (Furnishing fabrics often have printed writing down the sides which would show through otherwise.) Fold 2cm to wrong side down one trimmed edge, and pin the fabric, right side out, to the top ring. Work round the frame making 2cm wide pleats 2cm apart and pin each one securely to the frame. At the end of the first piece of fabric, lay it flat against the frame and start with a 2cm fold in the second piece, overlapping by exactly 2cm to make a pleat.

Continue in this manner until the whole circumference is covered.

5 Pinning the bottom ring
Space the pleats evenly round the bottom ring. If they need to be fanned out, ensure that they run at right angles to both the bottom and top rings.

Once the top and bottom rings are properly pinned, oversew as for the

lining. Trim away all excess material as close to the rings as possible.

6 Trimming the edges
Fold the leftover fabric along the diagonal, and cut out four lengths of 4cm wide bias strips. Using a steam iron or damp cloth, fold 5mm to the wrong side along both long edges.

Run thin lines of glue round the top and bottom outside edges of the rings. Repeat with glue on both folded edges of

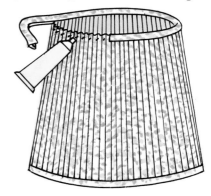

the trims. Gently position and ease into place. When joining on the second strip, turn under the raw end and lap this over the end of the first strip. Neaten the other end in the same way.

Simple lampshades

A fresh, new lampshade will instantly update your home furnishings. Shade-making is a craft which can be quickly and easily mastered, and professional results can be achieved in a very short time; the lampshades shown here can be

produced in an evening. The main advantage of making your own shade is that the decorating options are unlimited—you have a wide range of choice in materials and colours to co-ordinate with your own décor.

Before you begin

The simplest lampshades consist of a rigid covering supported by two interior metal rings. One of the rings contains the

Plain fabrics and floral and irregular, abstract patterns are all suitable for tapered shades, but large or geometric patterns are not. For cylinder shades you can use geometric and woven patterns as well.

fitting by which you attach the shade to the lamp. Rings are available in a range of diameters and fitting types; you can create many different lampshade shapes by varying the diameter of the rings and the shade height. The few special products needed for lampshade-making are available in craft shops, through mail-order handicraft suppliers, or in the haberdashery department of most department stores.

Lampshade bonding card is a stiff, self-adhesive backing to which a decorative outer covering is applied. Suitable choices for this purpose are closely woven lightweight cottons or cotton mixtures, gift wrapping or wallpaper. Dark or heavy materials such as hessian prevent the light from shining through, but can be effective for a quiet corner. Check your fabric over a light source to make sure how much illumination you will achieve. If you are making a tapered shade, select a small-patterned print or a plain colour—as the cut-out material is curved, a geometric or large pattern would look distorted. Iron-on bonding for

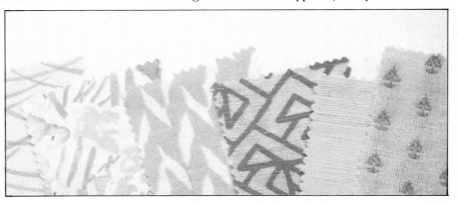

use exclusively with fabric can also be found, and a good time-saver, available from some stores, is fabric already fused to a firm backing, specially made for lampshade craft.

Trimmings

Shade edging is an important finishing touch. Select a trimming to enhance but not overpower the shade's appearance. A wide variety of home furnishing trimmings are available, including flat braid, fringe or pompon edgings, jumbo rick-rack or gathered frills. Velvet, grosgrain or satin ribbons are excellent for a tailored look, and bias binding readily conforms to the curves of the tapered shade.

General equipment

To make a shade, you will also need several large sheets of brown paper, pencil, metal ruler, string, set square, scissors, a drawing pin, trimming knife, scrap cardboard, masking tape, clear adhesive or white craft glue, and a few spring-clip clothes pegs.

Calculating amounts

To determine how much bonding card and covering material to buy, you must first make a paper pattern (see the instructions opposite). A cylindrical shade

has a rectangular pattern and the amount of bonding card is the same as the paper pattern. Add 2.5cm all round the pattern to get the measurements for the covering material.

Tapered shades have curved patterns. To calculate amounts of card and fabric, place pattern on a rectangular table top so that the corners of the small arc are flush with the table edge. Measure the distance between the pattern's widest points and from the edge of the table to the centre of the large arc, then add 2.5cm all round.

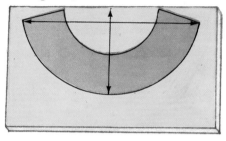

You must also buy sufficient self-adhesive cotton tape to fit around both the top and bottom ring, plus an allowance of 4cm for overlaps, and the

same amount of trimming to edge the top and bottom of the shade.

Making the pattern

A cylinder shade has a rectangular pattern. The short sides of the rectangle equal the shade height and the long sides equal the circumference of the rings plus a 1.5cm overlap. Mark off the rectangle's dimensions on the brown paper, using a set square for precise corners. Cut out, then test fit by clipping it to the rings with clothes pegs. Adjust if necessary.

The pattern for a tapered shade calls for some basic geometry. On a large sheet of brown paper, draw two parallel lines. Label the bottom line A and the top line B. The distance between these two lines equals the height of the shade.

Mark the centre of each line and fold the paper along these points. Use a set square to draw a perpendicular along the crease. Extend this line (C) upwards and downwards.

Measure the diameter of the bottom ring and mark off this distance on line A, centring line C between the points (label points D and E). Measure the diameter of

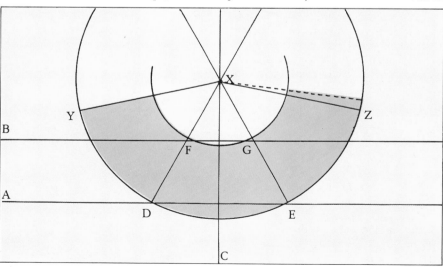

the top ring and mark it on line B in the same way (label points F and G).

Draw a line through F and D so that it crosses line C. Repeat for G and E. These lines will intersect line C at the same point (label this point X).

Improvise a pair of string-and-pencil compasses: fasten a piece of string to a drawing pin pivoting from centre point X. Draw a small arc passing through points F and G, then draw a large arc through points D and E.

Measure the circumference of the bottom ring with a piece of string, marking the points where the string meets. Lay the string on the large arc, the centre matching line C. Transfer the string points on to the arc (Y and Z). Draw lines from each of these points to X. For shade overlap, add 1.5cm at point Z and draw a line tapering towards point X.

The pattern, now complete, is indicated by the shaded diagram area. Cut it out and check fit with pegs as for cylinder pattern. Adjust if necessary.

The work area

If possible, work near an open window, as you will need good ventilation while gluing. Cover your work surface with a piece of cardboard, large enough to take the whole piece of covering material. Also make sure that you have all the general equipment you need to hand.

Materials

For a straight-sided drum shade, 35cm high
- ☐ 1 lampshade ring, 30cm in diameter, with fitting
- ☐ 1 plain ring, 30cm in diameter
- ☐ 40cm × 120cm wide bonding card
- ☐ 40cm × 122cm wide fabric
- ☐ 2m trimming for the edges (10cm main fabric will be sufficient to make a gathered frill as shown in the photograph on pages 48–9)

- ☐ 2m self-adhesive cotton tape

For a tapered shade, 25 cm high
- ☐ 1 lampshade ring, 30cm in diameter, with fitting
- ☐ 1 plain ring, 20cm in diameter
- ☐ 50cm × 120cm wide bonding card
- ☐ 1m × 122cm wide fabric
- ☐ 1.7m trimming for the edges
- ☐ 1.7m self-adhesive cotton tape

For a coolie shade, 18cm high
- ☐ 1 lampshade ring, 40cm in diameter, with fitting
- ☐ 1 plain ring, 10cm in diameter
- ☐ 50cm × 120cm wide bonding card
- ☐ 70cm × 122cm wide fabric
- ☐ 1.6m trimming for the edges
- ☐ 1.6m self-adhesive cotton tape

Making-up instructions

1 Applying cotton tape to the rings

Cut a piece of tape, the same length as the ring circumference plus 1.5cm. Press the adhesive side of the tape on to the outside

of the ring. Curl the tape round the ring, cutting slits to clear the prongs of the

fitting. Roll the tape round the ring and on to itself. Cover the second ring in the same way.

2 Mounting backing on to covering

Iron the fabric so that it is completely free of creases. (If you are using gift wrapping, use a cool iron on the wrong side.) Place the covering, right side down, on a flat work surface covered with a piece of clean cardboard; stretch taut, taping the edges to the surface. Peel back one edge of the protective backing so that you can align the bonding card with the covering material. Continue peeling the protective paper off the backing, gradually smoothing the adhesive side on to the covering fabric.

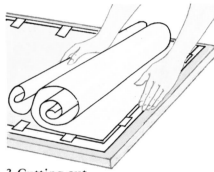

3 Cutting out

Lay the pattern on the bonded fabric so that its centre line matches the straight

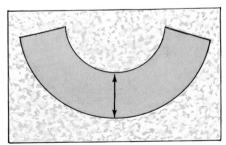

grain of fabric. Trace the outline on to the bonding card with pencil. Using a trimming knife, cut out the covering.

4 Fitting covering to rings

Tightly clamp the covering to the rings,

using clothes pegs. The rings belong just inside the top and bottom edges of the shade. Using a pencil, draw a line on the inside of the shade along the overlap. Remove pegs and rings.

5 Gluing shade join

Neatly spread a thin layer of clear adhesive between the pencil line and the

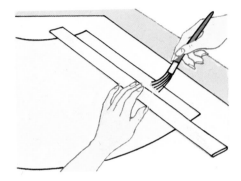

edge. Carefully press the edges together. Place a weight such as heavy tin cans or a bottle of wine over the full length of the join until the glue sets, which will take an hour or more.

6 Fixing coverings to rings

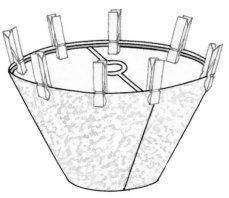

Place the tapered shade upside down on the table top. Run a line of glue round the narrow circumference, 3mm from the edge. Replace the large ring, holding it in place with pegs. Gently prod the small ring downwards until it reaches the glue line. Let it dry completely. Remove the pegs from the large ring and glue it in place, in the same way as for the small ring.

7 Attaching trimming

Cut lengths of decorative edging to fit the top and bottom shade circumferences, adding 2cm to each length for turnings. Glue trimming to the top and bottom edges, starting and ending on the shade join. Turn in and butt the edging ends.

If you trim your shade with bias binding which is lighter than the main fabric, it is advisable to back the binding with a strip of interfacing, the same width as the finished bias binding, to prevent the main fabric showing through. A suitable material for this is dressmaker's iron-on interfacing which can be cut on the bias and does not fray.

Decorative trimmings

The trimming adds the finishing touch to a lampshade. It can be elegant and sophisticated or pretty and cheerful. Choose a style that will match the room for which the lamp is intended.

1 Rick-rack edging looks festive and is easy to use in the bold jumbo size on shades that are either straight or tapered.

2 Velvet ribbon is a luxurious edging, suitable for a living room or bedroom. Choose a narrow width for tapered shades; it will conform more easily to the curved edges than wider ribbon. Two or three narrow ribbons in toning colours can be used together and will add an elegant finish to any shade.

3 Pompon fringe is a cheerful edging, only appropriate for the bottom edge, so select a matching braid for the top.

4 Scalloped frills can be made in the same fabric as the shade, or in a matching or contrasting plain fabric. Cut a bias strip, and turn under one raw edge a few mm and fold so that the folded edge overlaps the second raw edge. Press the fabric so that the join is at the centre back. Run a tacking line by machine, in a zig-zag pattern along the strip; pull up the bobbin thread to gather up the frill to the required length.

5 Gathered frills add a feminine touch; cut a strip and neaten the raw edges with a small zig-zag stitch. Place the strip on a length of lace trimming or broderie Anglaise, run a tacking line by machine along the centre of both fabrics and gather up.

6 Satin ribbon adds an elegant touch and can be used in combinations of toning colours in the same way as velvet ribbons. Use a narrow width for tapered shades.

7 Plaits can be made from cord or knitting wool in one colour only or in a combination of toning or contrasting colours, and will add a personal touch to a lampshade.

8 Broderie Anglaise with inserted ribbon makes a bright, cheerful trimming. Alternatively, for a feminine and romantic effect, insert a white or pale pastel ribbon into the broderie Anglaise and use lace or broderie Anglaise for the lampshade as well.

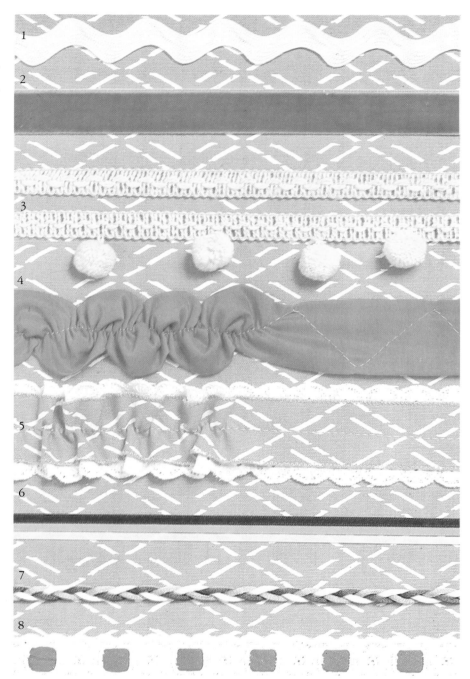

Pleated paper lampshade

Pleated lampshades are not difficult to make, but they require space and time. However, the results are so pretty and elegant that your efforts are well rewarded, and the materials you use can be purchased at very low cost. For safety reasons, it is recommended that a low-wattage bulb be used for this type of lampshade.

Before you begin

Two essential items of equipment are required before you can start work on a pleated shade: a conical frame and the right weight of card. If you intend using a particularly heavy type of wallpaper, and if the shade will be placed in a protected spot where it is unlikely to be banged or dented, you may be able to stiffen the paper by applying a few coats of wallpaper

Choose a wallpaper with a small abstract, geometric or floral pattern in pretty pastel colours.

size to the wrong side. Apply one coat at a time, allowing it to dry between applications and taking care not to allow any lumps to collect on the paper. If your paper is delicate, you should use a suitable weight of cartridge paper, and use a paper glue to bond your wallpaper before starting to cut out.

Very attractive plain-colour shades can be made using heavyweight cartridge paper in bright tones instead of wallpaper. Do not use fabric-backed lampshade card, as it is too stiff to pleat well and the paper is inclined to crack.

When using wallpaper, avoid one-way designs, as the paper will be cut out sideways. Choose small floral, geometric or abstract patterns.

General equipment

Coolie shades are the prettiest and most appropriate shapes for pleated covers. As they are fairly deep and the cut-out strips fairly long, you will also need a long ruler for marking out the paper—longer than the average 30cm size. To save money, you can use a piece of beading with a straight edge and the required measurements marked off with a pencil. A fairly sharp knife—not sharp enough to cut the paper, but fine enough to score a folding line—is also helpful. To make the holes for the securing trim, a proper hole-puncher makes a neat job, but if you are only planning to make one lampshade, a fine knitting needle used over a soft surface is almost as effective.

Trimmings

Pleated paper lampshades look best un-trimmed, as the wallpaper itself is busy enough to sustain a decorative effect. A pretty way to finish a shade is to use fine satin ribbon or lightweight cord to thread through the holes and tie the shade together. If you do decide to trim the edge of the shade, narrow grosgrain ribbon complements paper well and this type of ribbon is thick enough to be applied with a thin layer of fabric glue, with ends folded and butted.

Calculating amounts

The depth of the pleats can vary, but the deeper they are, the greater the play of light through the shade. You need a length of paper twice the wider circumference of the shade, and the width required is the depth of the shade, plus 2cm at the top and 3.5cm at the bottom to cover the rings.

Double the widest circumference measurement to calculate the length of ribbon required.

Taping a frame

To provide a base for stitching and to prevent rusting, all lampshade frames need to be taped before they are covered with fabric. Choose a loosely woven cotton tape, 7mm–11mm wide. A coolie shade like the one illustrated will require approximately 10m of tape.

Materials

For a coolie shade, 23cm deep and 40cm in diameter
- [ ] 1 coolie frame
- [ ] 10m lampshade tape
- [ ] 2 sheets plain white cartridge paper
- [ ] 1 roll of wallpaper or remnant, 250cm long and 28.5cm deep
- [ ] 3m × 3mm wide matching satin ribbon
- [ ] Paper glue

Making-up instructions

1 Applying tape to frame
Start the taping at the top join of a vertical strut. For ease of working, roll up a ball of tape, twice the length of the strut plus an extra allowance.

2 Working down the strut
Take a turn over the top rim and work down the strut, securing the end neatly as you wind the tape round the vertical strut.

3 Overlapping tape
Make sure you overlap each twist of the tape equally, to make a smooth line in the taping, and pull firmly between each twist so that the tape cannot unravel when it is stitched.

4 Finishing off
When you reach the bottom of the strut, make a figure-of-eight round the ring.

5 Stitching tape
Finish off the taping with a few neat stitches. Cut the end off close to the stitching.

6 Cutting the backing card
Cut the two sheets of cartridge paper to the same dimensions: each sheet will give you two narrow strips 28.5cm wide and 64cm long. Join these strips, overlapping the paper exactly 2cm (the width of the pleats) to make a total length of 250cm (twice the frame's wide circumference). Make final join after the paper has been pleated.

7 Mounting the wallpaper on the card
Lay the long strip of joined cartridge paper on top of the wrong side of a roll of wallpaper, matching the straight edge of the wallpaper to the bottom edge of the

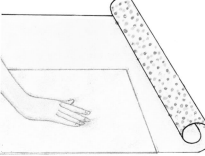

strip. Glue the card down with light pressure as you go, keeping to the straight edge all the time. Once firmly bonded, cut out the wallpaper to the exact size of the card.

8 Marking the pleat lines
Using a set square (or the square of the cartridge paper), mark the long strip on the cartridge paper side with parallel lines 2cm apart. These will mark the pleats.

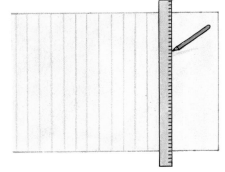

Do this carefully, even though it is laborious, as the finished effect depends on your accuracy at this stage.

9 Folding the pleats
Starting at one short edge, pleat up the

You don't need many materials to make pleated paper shades: just wallpaper or heavy cartridge paper, a frame, self-adhesive tape and ribbon.

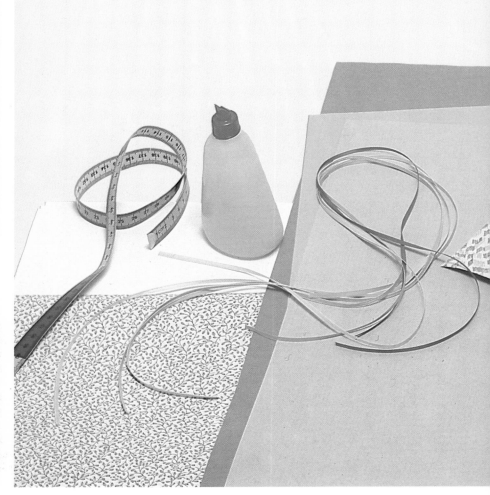

54

paper along the marked lines. Make sure than the folds fall exactly on your lightly pencilled lines: the lines themselves will not show in the creases when the shade is finished.

To make sharp pleats, always score along the lines marked, using a ruler and a knife to dent the paper. Once folded, run the flat side of the knife blade down each crease on the right side to make it really sharp.

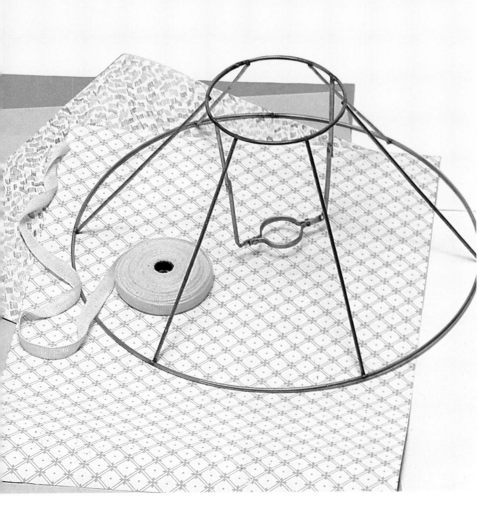

10 Making the holes

Using a hole puncher or knitting needle, mark two rows of holes in the centre of

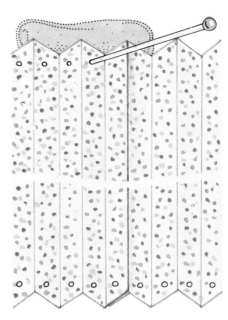

the pleats, 2cm from the top edge and 3.5cm from the bottom edge. Do this from the right side of the paper.

11 Threading the ribbon

Glue the final seam in the paper, overlapping the pleat so that the cut edge falls inside a pleat. Cut a length of satin ribbon, 1m long. Using a bodkin and starting at the final join, thread it through the holes at the top, 2cm from the edge. Gather up the pleats gently so as not to tear the holes until the pleats are almost touching. Repeat the process round the bottom of the shade, using a 2m long ribbon. Gather gently until the shade is approximately the same circumference as the frame. Drop the frame down into the shade and pull up the ribbons until they sit fairly tightly round

the frame. Tie each ribbon neatly in a little bow.

12 Stitching the shade to the frame

Using a double length of matching thread, loop-stitch round the rings of the

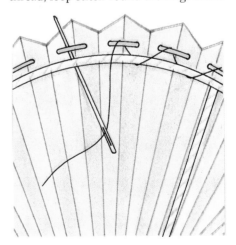

frame and the ribbons at the top and bottom, gently distributing the pleats evenly. Secure the thread with a few back stitches into the tape.

55

CHAPTER 4

Sitting pretty

There is barely a room in the home which will not benefit, in terms of both looks and function, from the addition of a chair or other form of seating.

From the kitchen to the bathroom, there is a vast choice of shapes and styles of chair. And you are by no means limited by what is on offer in the shops—a little know-how will enable you to turn even the tattiest-looking chair into a useful and attractive piece.

Of course, when you are planning seating, comfort must always be of prime consideration, and it is here that soft furnishing skills come in especially useful. Even the solidest of dining chairs or the soggiest of old sofas can be transformed with the right sort of cushions and padding.

Take a look round your home and consider the chairs which will suit your particular needs.

Welcome kitchen seating

In the kitchen, even if you do not have room for a table to eat at, it is lovely to be able to find room for a comfortable (but preferably not upholstered) armchair. For example, a traditional pine farmhouse chair, with slatted back, a copious seat and solid arms, with the addition of a couple of cushions, makes a welcoming and useful feature. It gives you somewhere to rest your feet when you're grabbing a few moments' peace over a cup of coffee, and a convenient place to sit and read recipes or check household bills. It also means that when you're slaving over a hot stove, family and friends will be more encouraged to linger and chat, rather than abandoning you for the comfort of your living room.

Dining room comfort

When it comes to seating, squab (shaped-seat) cushions, tied to the chair back, can transform solid, upright chairs into the sort of seating which will encourage guests to savour their meal.

With a little d-i-y, you can save your-

self a fortune. Pick up a selection of chairs from junk shops, paint them to match your décor, and add cushions to match your curtains—a mish-mash of shapes and styles can be turned into a smart set.

Living room ingenuity

The living room usually has the widest range of seating. Re-upholstery of sofas or suites is a fairly skilled task, but there is much you can do to improve the looks of seating in the sitting room without too much work or expense.

An Indian cotton bedspread thrown over a sofa and pinned (with safety pins) or fixed with touch-and-close fastener, makes an instant, no-sew transformation.

One of the latest looks in living room furnishings is the floppy, duvet look. This can be achieved with a little ingenuity: fold up an old duvet so it fits over an armchair, make a cover in a fairly tough material to help the duvet keep its shape, then throw it over the existing cover, so that the chair is swamped. Anchor with touch-and-close fastener.

As well as the main seating (and in modern homes, two neat sofas are often more compact and smarter-looking than the traditional sofa-and-two-armchairs arrangement) there is often room for occasional, more upright chairs in the sitting room, to accommodate extra guests. Again, the addition of seat

Loose covers in a pretty chintz fabric tie in nicely with a cottage-style furnishing scheme.

cushions or scatter cushions to match in with other furnishings both makes the chair more comfortable, and enables you to use fabrics to match those used elsewhere in the room, so that you have a well-planned, co-ordinated room, rather than an odd assortment of chairs.

Occasional chairs are also a nice place to show off hobbies. A tapestry seat—either a fitted, drop-in seat like the one shown on page 66, or a separate, shaped cushion—will last a lifetime on a chair which is only used occasionally.

For bathroom or bedroom

In the bathroom, why not take an old chair, paint it white (or a colour to match your bath) and make a towelling or PVC cover to fit the seat. This arrangement is very useful if there are older people in the house, who like to have somewhere to sit (the edge of the bath can be quite precarious) or if there are babies to be bathed and changed in the bathroom.

In the bedroom, you can go to town, dressing up a chair to suit the décor. Most people like to have an upright chair in the bedroom, on which they can hang jackets and lay out clothes for the following day, but it is also nice to be able to give the space to a small easy chair—somewhere you can sit quietly.

Chairs for children

With children going through so many stages from birth to adolescence, if you aren't careful you can easily spend a fortune on different seats at each stage. But there is usually a good market for second-hand seating for children, so pick up what you can cheaply, or borrow from friends and relations. With a little ingenuity you can ensure your children are always sitting comfortably without too much expense.

The first type of chair most babies move into is the bouncing cradle. The fabric cover of these cradles usually wears out long before the metal frame, so why not brighten up yours by following the instructions on page 67? Even if you don't feel up to a quilted, picture cover, you can recover the frame in a plain fabric to match nursery furnishings.

Another form of seating for babies is

When chairs or sofas are covered in a strongly patterned furnishing fabric, it's often better to have plain curtains, cushions and carpet, or a pattern that is substantially different in scale.

the swing-seat type of bouncer, which is fitted to the architrave in a doorway and can provide hours of entertainment. There is also the seat which is set into a circular trolley, helping to develop a child's sense of adventure. If you are re-making the seats for either of these sorts of chairs, you must ensure that the fabric, stitching and finishing are as strong as the original seat.

Later, children will move into high chairs and low chairs. Look out for high chairs which can be taken apart at a later stage to make a small chair and table. A padded seat makes a high chair more comfortable. Do ensure children can be firmly strapped in. You can economize on cost and space in the dining area by using a booster seat, fixed to an ordinary

Above and right: Pretty up the upholstery of a bedroom chair or box stool with a flounce which is either gathered or pleated, then add piping as the finishing touch. You could also cover a dressing table to match.

chair to turn it into a high chair when necessary.

With older children, a favourite form of seating is the sag bag, filled with poly-styrene granules, or piles of floor cushions. Children and the floor seem to have a magnetic attraction!

Try before you buy

Whatever type of chair you are buying, for whatever room in the house, do try it out as thoroughly as possible before

buying. Think about the use to which the chair will be put as you try it.

The two most common faults with chair design are that the seat is not deep enough and that there is not sufficient support for the small of the back. For relaxation, a high-backed easy chair is usually more comfortable, but less good-looking in most modern settings than low-backed sofas and chairs. If a chair is comfortable, you'll find there is less fidgeting and therefore less wear and tear

than in an awkwardly shaped chair where you are always on the move to find a comfortable position.

If the chair is for sitting in while you are eating or working, make sure it is the right height for the table or worksurface it is to go with.

Don't forget that elderly or arthritic visitors will have great difficulty in getting up out of some of the soft, sinking designs which are now so popular with the more agile.

59

Hammock

Hammocks conjure up pleasant thoughts of long, lazy days spent in the garden. This one is simple yet stylish, and quick to make, too. Canvas, rope and broom handles constitute the basic hammock; add a bright quilted panel and a soft pillow for comfort.

The hammock is for one adult or two children and has been designed with strength in mind: a double thickness of canvas forms the channels for the rope and poles, and double stitching is used where possible. The pillow is attached to the hammock with touch-and-close fastener to prevent it from slipping.

Before you begin

Hammocks are for sunny days so choose bright, zingy colours. Your choice of fabric for the quilted panel may be determined by the canvas available—often in

limited colours. Try to choose the canvas and furnishing cotton together so that the colours complement each other. A furnishing cotton with a cloud design has been used here for the padded section—other bold designs such as stripes, polka dots or rainbows would give the same effect.

To hang the hammock, use broom handles, 2cm in diameter, and 1cm diameter rope with a good breaking strain. The best choice of rope can be found at boat chandlers.

Calculating the amounts

Decide on the desired length and width of the hammock. To ensure strength, a double length of canvas is required, plus 20cm for the two channels for the broom handles, plus 5cm for seam allowances. Also buy a piece of canvas large enough for the top of the cushion.

For the quilted centre, buy a piece of

For the quilted top, choose bright colours and bold patterns for a really striking effect.

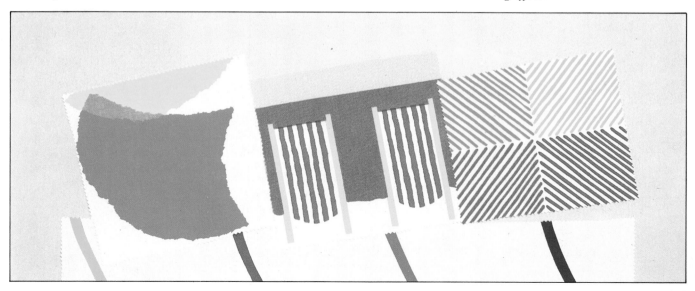

printed cotton fabric the length of the finished hammock, plus 5cm for turnings, allowing extra fabric to centre the design if necessary. Also buy a piece for the underside of the pillow and for the quilted centre.

You will also need medium-weight wadding to quilt the centre panel of the hammock and the pillow, plus a double thickness of the wadding for the pad in the pillow.

The broom handles need to extend at least 10cm outside each side, and the rope needs to be twice the length of the hammock, plus sufficient for hanging it in a suitable position.

Materials
For a hammock measuring 185cm long (including end channels) × 82cm wide, with a pillow 54cm × 40cm.
□ 4.20m × 86cm wide canvas
□ 2.30m × 122cm wide printed furnishing cotton
□ 2.20m × 110cm wide medium-weight wadding
□ 60cm touch-and-close fastener
□ Two broom handles, 120cm long
□ Strong sewing thread
□ Tailor's chalk
□ 16m strong rope

Making-up instructions

1 Quilting the centre panel
Cut out the centre panel, 180cm × 78cm, from printed fabric; cut out the wadding 2.5cm smaller all round. Lay the wadding out flat and place the fabric, right side up, on top. Fold the seam allowance of the fabric to the underside of the wadding; pin and tack in place all round.

Run horizontal and vertical tacking lines, approximately 10cm apart, through both layers to keep them firmly together while quilting. Pin and tack

around some motifs in the central part of the panel. Machine stitch around the designs. Alternatively, quilt by hand using a running stitch.

2 Preparing the canvas
Cut out a 375cm length of canvas. Lay it

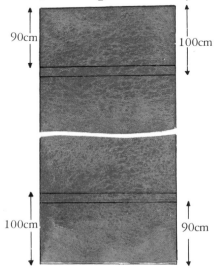

out flat, right side up, and mark the stitching lines for the channels 90cm and 100cm from each end.

3 Attaching the centre panel

Position the quilted panel between the stitching lines, leaving a 6.5cm wide

margin along each side. Pin and tack the panel to the canvas and topstitch all round 1cm in from the edge.

4 Attaching fastener

Cut a piece of touch-and-close fastener 4cm long. Pin and machine stitch one side of this centrally to the top end of the panel for attaching the pillow to the hammock. Place the top edge of the fastener against the topstitching.

5 Completing the quilting

Pin and tack around the remaining motifs to be quilted, through three thicknesses of material—canvas, wadding and printed fabric. Machine stitch around the designs, or sew by hand, if preferred.

6 Joining the ends of canvas

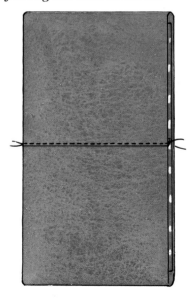

Lay the canvas out in one long strip with right side uppermost. Fold the ends to the middle with right sides together. Pin, tack and stitch the two ends together, taking a 2.5cm seam allowance. Press seam allowances to one side. Turn right side out and topstitch 5mm away from the seamline through three thicknesses of fabric for extra strength.

7 Stitching the side channels

Lay the hammock out flat with the seam at the centre of the underside. To make

the channels for the rope, turn 2cm of top and underside to the inside along each side; press. Run a double row of machine stitching close to this folded edge, starting and ending approximately 8cm from fold lines at head and foot. Make another row of stitching 3cm away and parallel to the first to form the channel.

8 Stitching the end channels

For the end channels, run a double row of

machine stitching across the hammock, about 5cm away from each fold line through both thicknesses of canvas. Insert the broom handles.

9 Inserting the rope

Cut the rope in half and thread one length through each side channel, leaving an equal amount free at each end for tying. Tie the rope to the broom handles at the head end. Pull the rope through the

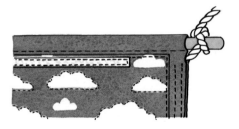

channels to gather the fabric slightly and form a pouch. When pulled up sufficiently, tie the other end of the rope to the other broom handle.

10 Preparing the pillow top

For the pillow, cut a piece of wadding 32cm × 46cm. Cut out a piece of printed fabric, 2.5cm larger all round, and place on top of the wadding, with right side uppermost. Fold the seam allowances over the edges of the wadding; pin and tack in place. Prepare for quilting in the same way as before.

Using plain canvas for the front of the pillow and printed fabric for the back cut out two pieces 45cm × 59cm. Centre the panel to be quilted on the plain fabric.

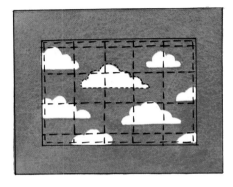

Pin, tack and machine stitch in place round the edges. Quilt around one motif through all three layers.

11 Attaching fastener
On the right side of the back of the

cushion, stitch the remaining strip of touch-and-close fastener 2.5cm down from the top edge and 2.5cm in from each side edge.

12 Finishing the pillow
Place the front and back with right sides together. Pin, tack and stitch, taking a 2.5cm seam allowance and leaving a 20cm opening along one side. Turn right side out and insert a double thickness of wadding. Slipstitch the opening to close and attach the pillow to the hammock.

13 Hanging the hammock
The best position for a hammock is between two tree trunks sturdy enough to take the weight of an adult. To secure the hammock well, use a round turn and two half hitches.

14 Making a round turn
Take the ropes from the end of the hammock and wind them round the tree

trunk twice. Holding the long end in your left hand and the short in your right, feed the ropes round the trunk until the

distance between the hammock and the trunk is right.

15 Making the first half hitch
Take the short end in front of and then behind the long end and come up

between the two turns round the trunk, making one hitch; pull tight.

16 Starting the second half hitch
Take the short end behind the long end.

17 Completing the second half hitch
Take the short end up and through the

loop, making the second hitch and pull tight.

63

Drop-in chair seats

Drop-in chair seats are a good first venture into the field of upholstery. Many dining chairs have loose seats and even if you have six to do it is not a big job. Suitable chairs can be bought at auctions and jumble sales, and with a little bit of work can be made to look very smart. These seats are not usually domed and can therefore be replaced with a sheet of foam.

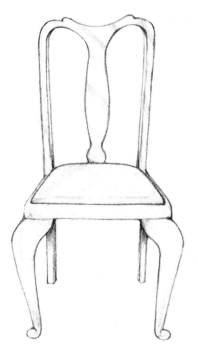

Before you begin
The old seat can be removed easily by pushing it up from underneath; the first step is to strip completely the old upholstery and remove all tacks. If your chair has been upholstered many times it may be necessary to fill the holes left by the tacks—do this with a mixture of sawdust and wood glue worked into a paste and smoothed across the tops of the holes with an old knife or putty knife. When the surface is dry, rub down with fine glasspaper until you have a smooth finish.

Suitable fabrics
Fabric should be chosen to blend with the style of décor and the style of the chair itself. Generally, most furnishing fabrics such as heavy cottons, chintz, velvet, heavy satins or textured fabrics can be used, but check before purchasing that it is recommended for the purpose; some fabrics like velvets are made only for curtaining as opposed to upholstering.

Plain velvet, woven patterns, cotton prints and striped fabrics are all suitable for chair seats.

Printed fabrics are easiest if the design selected is small, making the most economical use of fabric. For large patterns, try to centre the motif in the middle of the seat, and allow a bit extra when buying so that you can do this. It is also important to study the weight of the original fabric used and to buy a similar thickness for your new covers, otherwise the seat may not fit back into the frame.

Restoring the chairs
The method used will depend on the present finish of the chair. Some just need rubbing down with glasspaper; others can have the polish removed with white spirit. Usually most older chairs have some kind of thick varnish, polish or paint, which calls for a good paint stripper, a scraper, and a finishing rub with wirewool, and soapy water or turpentine (depending on whether the base coat is water or oil-based). The job can be messy, so use rubber gloves and work outside, if possible, to prevent the paint stripper from causing any damage.

Finish by washing off with water to remove all dissolved paint or varnish. Your chair may need to be lightly sanded down and can then be finished in a variety of ways: with varnish, polyurethane, oiling by rubbing in linseed oil, or polishing with a good wax polish to feed the goodness back into the wood. The colour of your chair can also be changed with wood stain before finishing, but it is always advisable to test first underneath the chair to check the colour.

Calculating amounts of fabric
Measure your seat frame from back to front and from side to side at the widest

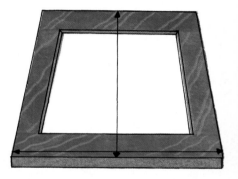

point and add 15cm to each measurement. This is the required amount of top fabric and calico for each chair. For the

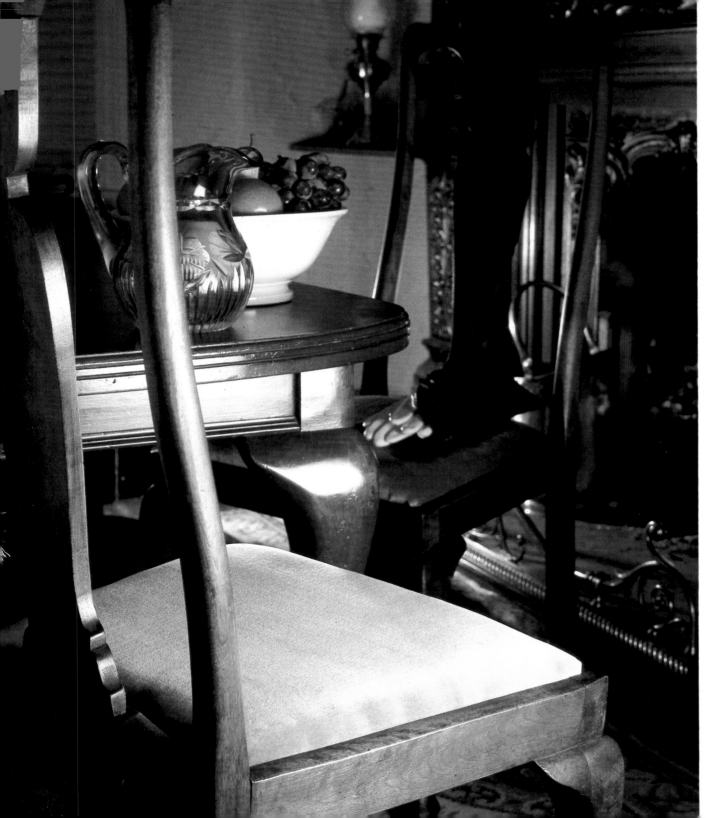

size of foam, take the original measurements and add 2.5cm to each. These measurements are given for a seat frame approximately 2cm deep but should your seat frame be deeper than this you will need to allow more fabric accordingly.

Materials
For two chairs
☐ 5m × 5cm wide webbing
☐ 15mm long upholstery tacks
☐ 2 foam rubber pieces 46cm square
☐ 60cm × 120cm wide calico
☐ 60cm × 120cm wide main fabric

Making-up instructions

1 Attaching webbing back to front
Fix three strips of webbing, equally

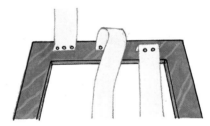

spaced, from front to back of the chair frame on the upper side, by turning the webbing back on itself.

2 Finishing vertical webbing
The webbing must be stretched as taut as possible and it is best if you have someone to help at this stage, one to stretch the

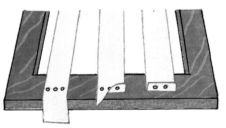

webbing and one to tack. Webbing can be stretched more tightly by pulling it over the edge of the frame and tacking before cutting the length. Once attached, trim off excess and turn back 1.5cm, tacking again in place.

3 Weaving webbing from side to side
Weave two strips of webbing across the chair under and over previous three

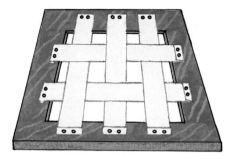

strips and fix in the same manner with tacks. It is easier to do the weaving part first before any tacking is done.

4 Cutting and shaping foam
Lay chair seat underside down on foam and mark around the edges with a felt-tip pen. Mark again 1.5cm outside this first

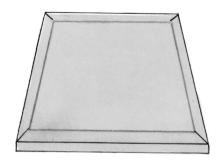

line and cut along it with scissors or a sharp knife. Bevel the edges of the foam between the inside line and the edge to half the depth of the foam.

5 Cutting and fixing calico cover
Lay foam, bevelled side down, on top of calico and mark all round 6cm away from the edge of the foam. Cut off the excess margin. Lay the seat frame top side down centrally on top of the foam. Fold calico over on to the back of the seat, pulling gently, and tack down in the centre of the

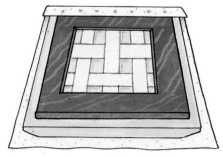

wood frame. Continue tacking at intervals of about 3.5cm to within 7.5cm of the corner. Repeat with the front edge but check the tension of the calico before tacking. The edges of the seat should be gently rounded. If you pull the fabric too tight the rounded edge will be bumpy between the tacks. Follow this method to complete the front and sides of the seat.

6 Pleating seat corners
There is no standard way to arrange the corners as this varies from chair to chair.

You will need to be patient and pleat the corners in the best way for your chair, remembering that most of the pleating

will be hidden by the seat frame. It is best to start by gently pulling the corner piece over the back of the seat and forming little pleats on each side, tacking in place through all the layers of fabric. Excess fabric can be cut away since bulk should be avoided wherever possible, or the seat may not fit comfortably into the frame.

7 Fitting the top cover
Allow 7.5cm around the edges of the seat so that the top cover will cover up the calico on the reverse side, and avoid the previous line of tacks to give a better finish. The top cover is fixed in exactly the same way as the calico but without pulling the fabric since the rounded edges

have already been shaped and held by the calico. Keep the cover fabric fairly taut

and smooth. Trim off excess fabric at the corners. Your seat is now ready to drop into the chair frame.

A needlepoint cover can be used instead of fabric for a drop-in seat.

Bouncing baby seat

This charming chair will keep your baby safe and happy whether out in the garden or indoors. It consists of a metal frame covered with quilted fabric decorated with a colourful appliqué design.

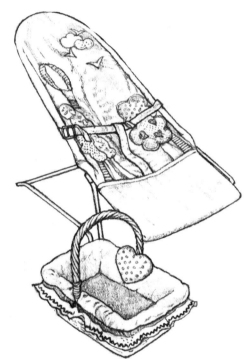

Before you begin

A strong, washable fabric such as canvas, calico, furnishing cotton, denim or corduroy is required for the cover, and

Choose a dark background fabric and stripes, checks and small prints in bright colours for the appliqué.

quilted fabric works well too. Choose a small pattern such as a polka dot or a plain fabric for the background and brightly coloured scraps of cotton for the appliqué motifs.

A lighter weight fabric can also be used if a layer of lightweight wadding is sandwiched between two layers of fabric. Wash all fabrics before cutting out to prevent shrinkage later and choose synthetic wadding for the same reason.

Calculating amounts

If you have the old cover, simply unpick and measure the pieces to estimate the amount of fabric required. Alternatively, measure the frame in the following way: from the head to the bottom of the seat section where it joins the foot rest, and from side to side at the widest point. Add

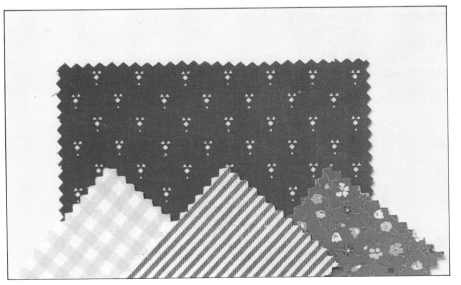

3cm to the length for seam allowances and 16cm to the width for channels encasing the frame and a dart at the bottom to form the seat. (Allow a bit extra round the head section and sides for ease of working.) Measure the length and width of the foot rest; double the length and add 3cm for seam allowances; add 5cm to the width for seam allowances.

The top edge is kept in place with a pocket; allow 20cm for the length and the same width as for the main piece.

You will need two pieces of fabric and one piece of wadding for each section.

For the basket liner, measure the length and width of the base of the basket and add 1.5cm all round for seam allowances. For the gusset, measure the circumference and allow 1½ times this measurement for fullness. The depth of the gusset should equal the height of the basket, plus 7.5cm for overhang and casing, plus 1.5cm for seam allowances. You will also need a frill 7cm wide and the same length as the gusset, plus the same length of ric-rac braid and white cotton tape.

Making the baby chair

Materials
- ☐ 1.50m × 122cm wide cotton fabric
- ☐ 1m × 90cm lightweight synthetic wadding
- ☐ One 3cm wide buckle
- ☐ Scraps of brightly coloured cotton fabric
- ☐ Matching sewing threads
- ☐ Dressmaker's graph paper
- ☐ Tissue paper

1 Cutting out the main section
Cut out one piece of fabric according to the above measurements. Fold in half lengthways with right sides together; pin and tack a 20cm long dart from the fold to the bottom edge 5cm away from the fold.

Place the fabric on the frame, right side outwards, and fold the side edges round the frame up to the point where it starts to curve; pin in place and mark the stitching lines with tailor's chalk on both back and front of the fabric. Trim the fabric to size, leaving a 1.5cm seam allowance round the top edge and along the bottom, and remove from the frame. Use this piece when cutting out the second fabric piece and the wadding. Stitch the dart on all three pieces.

2 Working the appliqué design

Using dressmaker's graph paper, enlarge the motifs to the right size and cut out the pattern pieces. Cut out appliqué motifs from brightly coloured fabrics. Place one main piece on the frame and arrange the appliqué motifs on the fabric to produce a

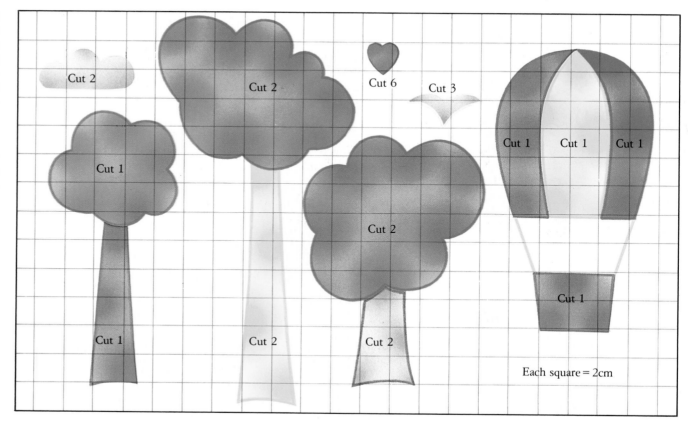

Cut 2
Cut 2
Cut 6
Cut 3
Cut 1
Cut 1
Cut 1
Cut 1
Cut 1
Cut 1
Cut 2
Cut 2
Cut 2

Each square = 2cm

pleasing design; pin in place. Remove the cover from the frame, tack and stitch with a wide, close zig-zag with matching threads.

3 Stitching the side channels

Place the three main pieces together,

right sides of fabric outwards and wadding in between. Ensure that the darts match exactly. Tack the layers together at 10cm intervals and round the edges. Turn 5mm to the wrong side along each edge; pin and tack. Place on frame again to check fit. Remove and pin, tack and stitch the channels, ending 10cm above the foot section. Trim wadding so that it tapers towards the top of the foot rest. Turn under raw edges, enclosing the wadding and slipstitch to close.

4 Preparing the pocket

Using the top end of one main piece as a pattern, cut out two pieces of fabric and one of wadding, 20cm long. Place the

two fabric pieces with right sides together and put the wadding on top; pin and tack

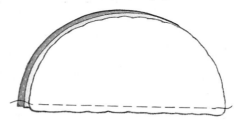

along the straight edge. Place a piece of tissue paper on the wadding and stitch by machine 1.5cm from the straight edge. Trim the seam allowances and then turn right side out.

5 Finishing the head section

Place the pocket piece on the right side of the main piece; pin, tack and stitch round

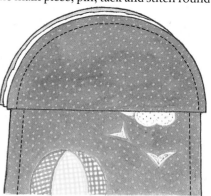

the curved edge 1.5cm from the raw edges, tapering towards the side edges where the hood overlaps the side channels. Trim seam allowances and zig-zag stitch together to neaten.

6 Preparing the foot rest

Cut out two pieces of fabric and one of wadding for the foot rest. Place the two fabric pieces with right sides together and the wadding on top. Place a piece of tissue paper on the wadding and stitch round three edges, leaving one short edge open. Ensure that the width of the foot rest is the same as the bottom of the main section, plus 1cm at each side. Trim seam allowances and turn right side out.

7 Joining the foot rest to the main section

Place the foot section on the main section, right sides together and raw edges matching. Let the foot section extend 1cm outside each edge of the main sec-

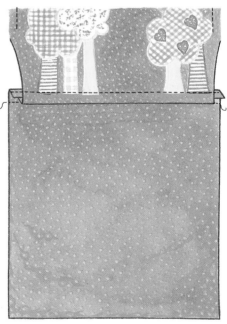

tion. Pin, tack and stitch together 1.5cm from the raw edges. Trim the seam allowance of the main section to 5mm; fold the other one over it so as to enclose all raw edges. Pin, tack and stitch again.

8 Finishing the foot rest
Fold the foot rest to the right side until it meets the seam. Pin, tack and stitch the

sides together, taking a 1cm wide seam allowance. Turn right side out.

9 Quilting
Using a thread that matches the background fabric, work a line of running stitch all round each appliqué motif, just outside the edge, through all layers.

10 Making straps
Cut three 7cm wide strips, 12cm, 27cm and 50cm long, from the remaining fabric. Fold each strip in half lengthways, right side inwards. Pin, tack and stitch 1cm from the long edge. Turn right side out. Turn under raw edges by 5mm at each end and slipstitch to close. Turn under 1cm at one end of the longest strap and position it at the back of the main

piece, on the seamline, 20cm up from the foot rest. Pin, tack and stitch in place. Fold the shortest strap in half round the buckle and attach to the opposite side in the same way. Turn under one end of the third strap 1cm, then 4cm and stitch close to the edge to form a loop. Attach other end as before to centre of bottom edge. Thread long strap through loop.

Making the basket liner

Materials
- □ 40cm × 90cm wide cotton fabric
- □ 20cm × 90cm wide contrasting fabric for the frill
- □ 1.50m ric-rac braid
- □ 1.50m white cotton tape
- □ Matching sewing threads
- □ Scraps of cotton fabric and ric-rac braid for pin cushion
- □ Small amount of filling

1 Preparing the gusset
Cut out two strips of fabric, 75cm × 20cm. With right sides together, join short edges at both ends, leaving 9cm

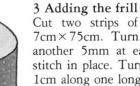

unstitched towards one long edge. Press seams open and continue pressing the seam allowances to the wrong side along the slits. At the same long edge, turn under 5mm and then 2cm; pin in place. At the opposite edge, run a double row of gathering stitches 1.5cm from the raw edge.

2 Joining the gusset to the base
Cut out the base and, with right sides together and raw edges matching, place the gusset on the base, pulling up the gathering threads to make gusset the right length. Pin, tack and stitch all round, 1.5cm from the raw edges.

3 Adding the frill
Cut two strips of contrasting fabric, 7cm × 75cm. Turn under 5mm, then another 5mm at each short edge and stitch in place. Turn under 5mm, then 1cm along one long edge, pin and tack. Place a length of ric-rac braid over the tacking line and stitch in place through all layers of fabric. Run a double row of gathering stitches along the opposite long edge, 5mm from the edge. Pull up the gathering threads until the frill is the same length as the gusset. Insert the gathered edge into the casing; repin, tack and stitch close to the edge, attaching the frill and making the casing simultaneously. Cut the cotton tape in half and thread one half through each casing. Place the liner in the basket and tie bows round the handle at each side.

4 Making the pin cushion
Enlarge the heart shape from the graph and cut out the pattern. Cut out two pieces of fabric and two lengths of ric-rac braid. With right sides together and ric-rac sandwiched in between, pin, tack and stitch together, leaving an opening along one side. Insert the filling and then slipstitch to close.

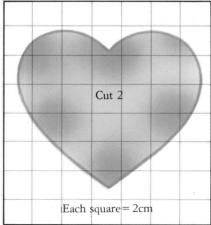

Cut 2

Each square = 2cm

Padded wicker chair

With this charming padded chair cover, turn a simple wicker chair into a comfortable and decorative piece of furniture which will add interest to your home.

Before you begin

Use a plain cotton or polyester/cotton as the background for the appliqué; choose a pale blue for the back and a green for the cushion. The piping is made in emerald green. Cotton, polyester/cotton and lawn are suitable for the appliqué motifs; it is advisable to use fabrics of similar weight for best results. Choose plain and printed greens for the fields, hedge and tree in pale, medium and dark shades. Plain, green fabrics are best for the hills, white for clouds and brown for the tree trunk.

Making the pattern from the chair

Tape together a few sheets of newspaper and place this inside the back of the chair so that it covers the required area; fix with adhesive tape. Using a felt-tip pen, draw round the area to be padded. Trim the paper roughly to size and try the fit on the chair. Trim again if necessary. Repeat for the cushion area.

Calculating the amounts

Measure the length and width of the pattern for the back, adding 5cm all round to allow for turnings and shrinkage. You will need this amount of wadding and twice this amount of fabric. Measure the cushion pattern in the same way. Again you will need this amount of

Use blue and white for sky and clouds and a selection of plain and patterned greens for tree, hedge, fields and hills.

wadding, and twice this amount of fabric, plus 20cm extra for the gusset, and a 5cm thick foam pad.

To estimate the amount of piping cord required, measure the back pattern from the base at one side all round to the base at the other side and then measure the circumference of the cushion pattern.

Materials

- ☐ 2m × 90cm wide pale blue poplin
- ☐ 1m × 90cm wide pale green poplin
- ☐ 50cm × 90cm wide emerald green cotton
- ☐ 40cm × 90cm wide dark green patterned cotton for the hedge
- ☐ Scraps of plain and patterned cottons as follows: six different green patterns for tree foliage, brown for tree trunk, white for clouds, five different plain greens for hills and eleven different

plain and patterned green fabrics for fields

- ☐ One embroidery marker pen
- ☐ Four packets of paper-backed bonding
- ☐ 4m × No. 2 piping cord
- ☐ 4m × 1.5cm pale green satin ribbon

- ☐ Matching sewing threads
- ☐ One foam pad 45cm × 50cm × 5cm
- ☐ 1.5m medium-weight wadding
- ☐ Dressmaker's graph paper

Making-up instructions

1 Enlarging the design

Using dressmaker's graph paper, enlarge the appliqué motifs and the back and cushion sections shown on pages 74–5, and cut out the pattern pieces. If your chair is different, adapt the appliqué design to suit your own pattern.

2 Arranging the appliqué on the back

Cut out a piece of the pale blue poplin for the chair back, adding 5cm all round your pattern to allow for shrinkage when the fabric has been quilted. Cut a piece of wadding to the same size.

Trace the appliqué motifs on to the paper-backed bonding. Cut out the shapes and iron on to the relevant fabrics. Mark the name and/or number of each shape for identification later. Cut out the fabric motifs carefully.

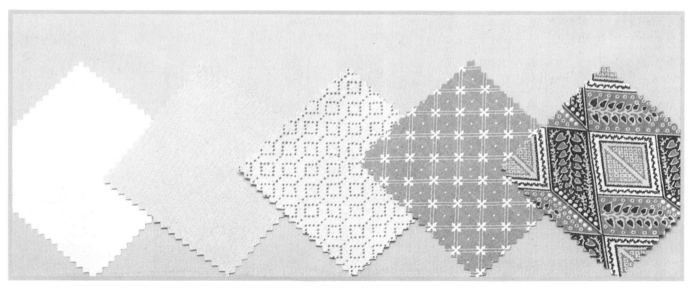

Following the design, position and iron the hills on to the back piece one by one, in numerical order, overlapping the edges as indicated. Next iron on the two hedge pieces to cover the lower raw edges

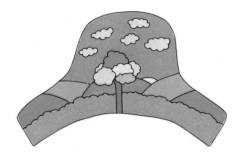

of the hills. Butt the sides of the hedges together and cover the join with the tree trunk. Iron on the tree foliage shapes one by one, in numerical order, overlapping as necessary. To complete the design, iron on the clouds in a pleasing arrangement, so that they are fairly evenly distributed over the sky.

3 Quilting the back

Using the embroidery pen, mark parallel lines on some hills and random wavy lines on other hills. Also draw in the radiating lines in the sky using a ruler. Place the back piece, right side up, on the wadding and tack the layers together vertically and horizontally, starting at the centre and working outwards. Using a straight, medium-length machine stitch, sew along the marked lines on the hills in various green threads. Stitch the sky lines in the same way in pale blue. Each line of stitching should go right to the raw edge, and the ends should be tied together and cut off. They will be covered by the machine satin stitch.

For the machine satin stitch, set your machine on a very close, fairly wide zig-

zag stitch, and sew all round the raw edges of the hills in numerical order, using the same green thread for all of them. Stitch along the top of the hedge in a different green, and around the tree trunk in brown. Stitch the tree foliage shapes in different greens, following the

numbers. Stitch all round the clouds in white. You can vary the width of the satin stitch to enhance the design. For example, use a wider stitch on the hedge in the foreground and narrower on the tree and clouds. However, make sure that the raw edge is covered each time—this can be tricky if you are using a narrow stitch.

4 Piping the edge

Try the quilted back piece in the chair, taping it in place. Mark lightly with the embroidery pen the finished edge through the wickerwork. Check with your pattern and outline the finished size. Trim the quilted fabric to 2cm outside this line all round. Zig-zag stitch all round this edge.

Cut 3cm wide bias strips from the emerald green fabric and make up 4m of

piping. With raw edges matching, place the piping on the right side of the quilted back piece, up the sides along the top;

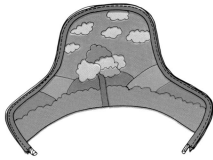

pin, tack and stitch all round close to the piping cord.

5 Finishing the back piece

Cut another piece of pale blue poplin the same size as the quilted piece. With right sides together and raw edges matching, pin, tack and stitch the front and back together along the previous stitching line, leaving a gap in the stitching along the lower edge as indicated on the pattern. Turn right side out and press. Turn in raw edges and slipstitch.

Remove all marks made by the embroidery pen with a watercolour brush dipped in clean water and leave to dry; all traces of the ink will disappear.

6 Sewing on ribbon ties

Try the padded backing in the chair and mark about 12 suitable points for ties to go round the wickerwork. Cut the satin ribbon into 12 equal lengths and stitch by hand to the padded back piece at the positions marked.

7 Fitting the foam cushion pad

Using your paper pattern, cut the foam pad to shape. Tie the padded back piece in position inside the chair, place the foam

pad on the seat and make any necessary adjustments.

8 Making the cushion appliqué

Cut a piece of pale green poplin and a piece of wadding, each 5cm larger all round than the paper pattern. Cut out and back the field pieces in the same way as for the back appliqué motifs. Remove the backing paper and position the pieces on the green poplin, making sure to butt them together exactly; carefully iron the fields in place.

Lay the fabric, right side up, on the wadding and tack the layers together as before. Mark quilting lines as indicated in the pattern; straight stitch along these lines in different colours. Satin stitch round the fields as before to cover the raw edges, using the same colour thread throughout.

Begin satin-stitching the short lines between fields 1 and 2, 10 and 11, and 8 and 9. Then stitch the longer vertical lines and finish with the horizontal lines above and below fields 4, 5 and 6.

9 Piping the cushion top

Lay the foam pad on top of the wrong side of the quilted piece and, using a well-sharpened pencil, draw all round it to indicate the stitching line. Trim the fabric to 1cm outside this line. Cut

another piece of poplin to this size. Zig-zag stitch all round the raw edges of the quilted piece.

With right sides together and raw edges matching, pin, tack and stitch the remaining length of piping to the quilted piece. Overlap the piping where the ends meet and trim away excess cord from inside to avoid bulk and make a flat join.

10 Completing the cushion cover

From the pale green poplin, cut 7cm wide strips and join together to make one continuous gusset strip long enough to go round the cushion, plus 2cm. With right sides together, raw edges matching and piping sandwiched in between, pin the strip round the edge of the quilted piece. Stitch the two short ends together, taking a 1cm seam allowance, and then stitch the gusset strip in place close to the piping cord.

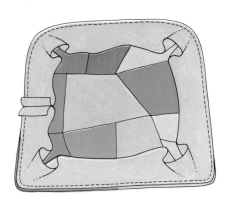

With right sides together and raw edges matching, stitch the base piece to the gusset, leaving an opening along the back edge. Notch the seam allowances at the corners, turn right side out and then press.

Insert the foam pad, turn under the raw edges and slipstitch to close. Place the cushion on the chair.

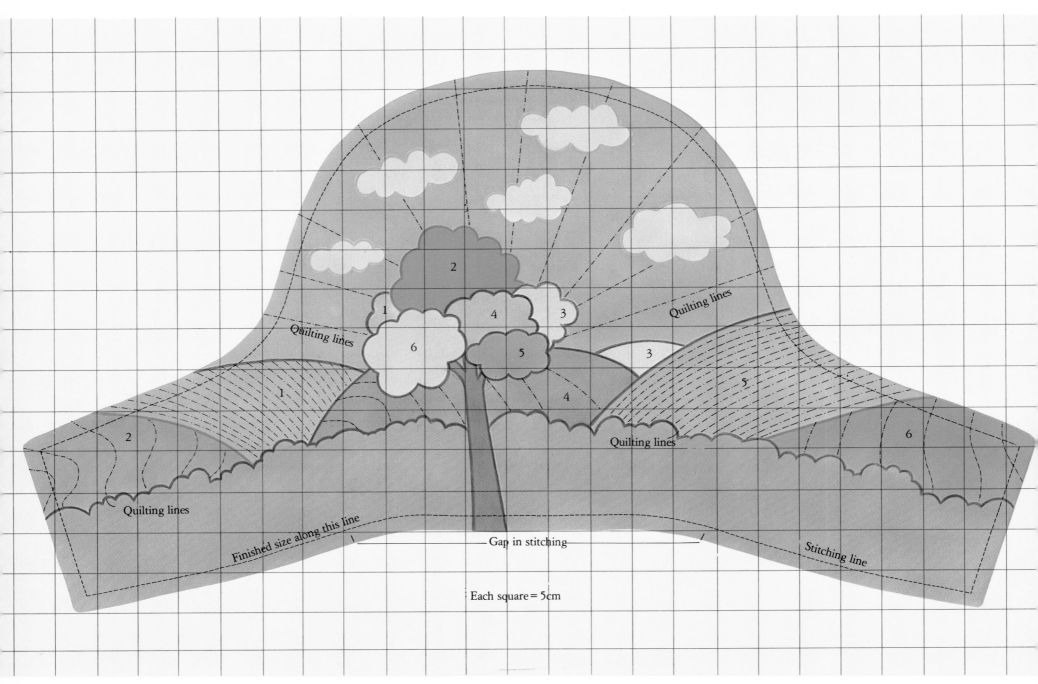

2

1

2

4 3

1

6

5

3

Quilting lines

Quilting lines

4

5

Quilting lines

2

6

Quilting lines

Finished size along this line

Gap in stitching

Stitching line

Each square = 5cm

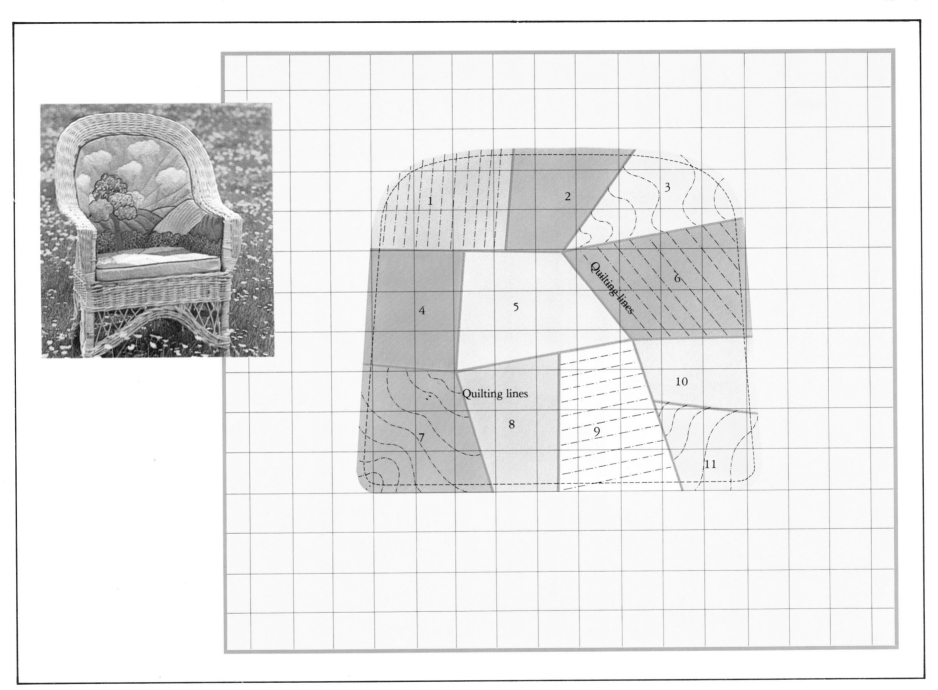

CHAPTER 5

Curtains up

The way in which you dress your windows—curtains, blinds,
sheers or a combination of these—is one of the main
statements of style in any room.

The choice of window dressing is unlimited. Looking at curtains alone, you can, for example, choose full, long, velvet curtains for a traditionally furnished room; a light layer of clean, sheer curtains to screen the window and diffuse the light in a modern room; or short, chintzy curtains, complete with frills and tiebacks for a country cottage look.

And the curtains can be used to play tricks with the proportions of the windows. Full, floor-length curtains, set outside the window frame, lend importance to an otherwise plain window. Layers of café curtains and a blind can break up the shape of a tall, upright window. Curtains set inside the recess give definition to its shape.

Choosing fabric

Unless you are creating a particular effect, choose your fabric from the wide range of furnishing fabrics available, which include plain or printed cotton, synthetic fibres woven to look like silk or linen, velvet, hessian, and linen or linen union.

Choose fabrics according to other furnishings in the room. Unless you are confident when it comes to colour scheming and co-ordinating patterns, go for plain fabrics if there are other patterned surfaces such as wallpaper, upholstery or carpet. Conversely, if the room has a lot of plain surfaces, you can happily choose patterned curtains.

Manufacturers have made co-ordination easy by producing ranges of matching or toning wallpapers and fabrics, so that you can achieve designer effects with a minimum of work by selecting fabrics that are designed to go together. Furnishing fabrics are generally fade-resistant, which is important for curtains, and come in wide widths so that fewer seams are necessary.

Café curtains may be hung either inside or outside the window recess and may be as high or low as you like.

When buying, drape the fabric so that you can see how it will look when it is hung—the effect is often quite different. For example, large, pictorial patterns may be lost when made up into curtains. Stand well back so that you can check the effect as you will see it in your room—you will be looking at the curtains from the door, the armchair or the bed, not from arm's length.

If you are choosing plain fabric, think about the texture. There are no hard and fast rules, but you probably won't want to put a rough, country hessian fabric with a velvet-pile carpet, for example, whereas hessian can give an attractive rustic flavour when combined with a berber-type carpet.

Your curtains will probably provide one of the main areas of colour in a room, so choose the colour carefully. Remember that the colour will look different, according to the light it is in. In the shop, fabrics are often displayed under harsh strip lights. The effect will change when you take the fabric to the daylight, and change again when you look at it under the soft light of a table lamp, as it will be seen in the evenings, when your curtains are most on show.

It's a good idea to buy half a metre or a metre of fabric before making your final decision. Take it home and look at the effect in all kinds of light, checking the colour against existing furnishings before making your final decision. You can use the sample to make up cushions or other accessories once you have made your decision.

Lining curtains

It is always a good idea to line curtains, unless you are going for a particular effect

which is better without lining. Linings help to insulate the room when the curtains are closed—against noise coming in and heat going out. The lining will also help the curtain to hang better, and prolong the life of the curtain by protecting it from the sun and the dirt which inevitably penetrates any window.

Detachable linings are a good idea. They are attached to a heading tape which loops on to the hooks holding the curtain. You can wash the lining when the curtains need cleaning, thus reducing the weight at the dry cleaners. But a detachable lining is not really necessary with washable curtains, unless they are so large that they would be difficult to fit into the machine with attached linings.

Another point in favour of lining curtains is that you can choose lining

Left: A smocked heading is well suited to cottagey check gingham. Above: Combining full-length and café curtains can look very striking and unusual.

fabric of the same colour throughout the house, to give a uniform look to the outside of the house.

Interlining is a professional touch which adds extra body to curtains, giving them a very luxurious look. An interlining of soft fabric, such as bump or flannelette, is stitched to the curtain between the outer fabric and the lining.

Headings and tracks

Before you can make your own curtains, you will have to decide on the size they are to be, and you can't do this until you have decided on the type of track and the type of heading (or gathering) that you want at the top.

Most curtains are gathered at the top by means of a special tape which is stitched to the curtain. Cords running through it are drawn up to give the fullness and special effects. The simplest tape is a standard heading tape, suitable for small, lightweight curtains or for headings hidden beneath a pelmet or valance. Pencil-pleated heading tapes give a crisper, more formal, finish to the curtains, stiffening the top few inches of the curtain as well as gathering them. You can also buy tapes which give special effects, such as smocking-like gathers or pinch pleats.

Pinch pleats may also be formed with specially designed pocketed tapes. Curtain hooks with 'hands' of prongs are slipped into groups of pockets to make up double or triple pleats. This type of finish is more versatile than a corded tape, as you can choose how many hooks to use and adjust the fullness and width, but it is more fiddly to work out and finish.

Although headings are now usually machine-stitched, they were traditionally stitched by hand, and this technique has to be used for the style of café curtains shown on page 84.

The heading tape you choose dictates the fullness of the curtain. With standard tape you will have to make the curtain at least one and a half times wider than the width of the curtain once the tapes are drawn up. Other headings require two to three times the drawn-up width.

Decide what type of track you want and where to position it. Simple plastic tracks can be fitted inside or outside the window recess, to the ceiling, the wall, the window frame or a special wooden batten fixed above the window. The heading tape and hooks can be positioned so that the top of the curtain conceals the track. Or you may prefer to make a feature of the tracks by using a wooden or brass pole (in which case remember to check whether your heading will require longer-necked hooks).

In smaller windows, the curtain can be finished at the top with a simple casing which slots on to a wire or slim pole.

Blinds

Blinds are often an economical way to screen a window. Ready-made bamboo or bamboo and paper blinds are one of the cheapest options available, and roller blinds are easy to make from a kit.

One of the most popular types of blind is the flounced, Austrian or festoon blind. It has a heading like a curtain, but this is kept permanently closed, with the blind fixed to endstops at both ends of the track. Cords running down the curtain draw up the blind in flounces.

Roman blinds give a crisper, more architectural effect. They are flat blinds which are drawn up into deep folds by cords running down the back.

A festoon blind adds luxury and elegance to any room.

Festoon blind

Festoon blinds are very decorative and look extravagant; the soft, scalloped effect can bring a feminine touch to any room. They hang from a curtain track and are drawn up by ring cords. When festoons are raised the blind is ruched up into soft gathers.

Before you begin

When you pick a curtain heading tape, make sure that it suits the fabric and the room setting: for example, a pencil pleat tape looks good in a fairly elegant room, but a simpler tape would look better used on sheer fabrics. You can add frills or a lace edging to the sides and base of your blind or bind the edges in a contrasting colour.

Suitable fabrics

Festoon blinds look particularly attractive in bedrooms and living rooms. Floral cotton prints and seersucker will produce a gentle, decorative effect, whereas bold graphic patterns will not harmonize well with the soft lines of festoons.

Traditionally, festoon blinds—or Austrian blinds, as they are sometimes called—are made of fairly light fabrics, which are left unlined.

Luxurious fabrics such as moiré, taffeta, satin and chintz, in plain, rich colours, will look elegant and dramatic in large windows.

Festoons are also a good alternative to nets to give an opulent look, for instance, in bathrooms. Make them up in voile using a lightweight tape.

Curtain tape

For the curtain heading, choose pencil pleat or standard curtain heading tape.

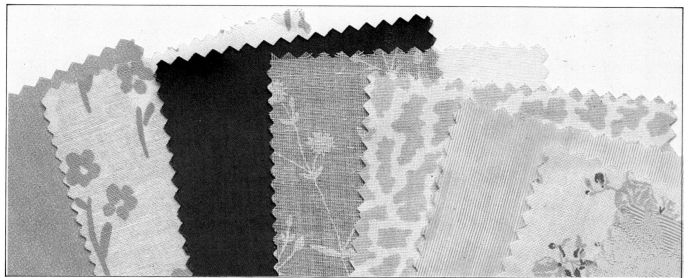

The length should be the same as the full width of the ungathered blind plus 3cm for neatening.

Ordinary white cotton tape is appropriate for the vertical gathers. You will need the length of the blind by the number of tapes you want (see step 7). Make sure that the tapes are straight and equally spaced across the back of the blind.

To avoid visible seams on the right side of the blind, iron the tapes on to the blind using double-sided bonding tape. Follow the manufacturer's instructions carefully.

Cord

This is used for pulling up the gathers and is threaded through the rings at the back of the blind. White nylon cord is strong, but fairly thin, and will not show through.

Estimate the amount you should buy by allowing 2½ times the length of each vertical tape.

The curtain track

The track should be fixed to a batten (which you can buy from a timber merchant) so fix one above your window before you hang your blind.

Materials

For a festoon blind 90cm wide (without the frill) and 2.25m long you will need:
- [ ] 6m × 120cm wide fabric
- [ ] 18m of bias binding
- [ ] Matching sewing thread
- [ ] 2.5m of curtain heading tape
- [ ] Curtain hooks
- [ ] 9m of white cotton tape
- [ ] 26 white plastic curtain rings
- [ ] 22m of white nylon cord
- [ ] One 90cm 50 × 25mm wooden batten
- [ ] 4 picture ring screws
- [ ] 1 cleat

Floral cottons, pretty sheers and chintzes, and elegant moirés, satins and damasks go beautifully with the soft scallops of festoon blinds.

Measuring the window

When measuring your window, always use a wooden metre stick or steel measure—this will ensure accurate measurements. Decide whether you want the blind to hang inside or outside the reveal. For a blind hanging inside the

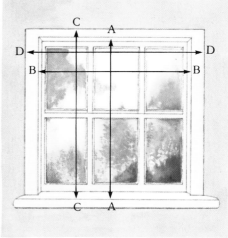

reveal, measure the inside length and width (A and B as shown). When measuring for a blind hanging outside the reveal (C and D), extend the blind width by at least 5cm on each side. You will need two or 2½ times the width in fabric to achieve the right fullness, the exact amount depending on your heading tape. The length is the same as the length of the window, plus approximately 20cm. Also allow enough fabric for the frills.

Making-up instructions

1 Cutting lengths of fabric

Cut the fabric into as many lengths as necessary in order to gain the correct width, making sure that the fabric grain is straight and when stitched together the design will match.

2 Joining fabric pieces with a French seam

Place the two pieces of fabric to be joined with the wrong sides together. Pin and

tack 1.5cm from the edge. (This line will be the final stitching line.) Stitch 6mm outside the tacked line.

3 Completing the French seam

Remove the tacking stitches. Press the seam open. Trim down the seam allow-

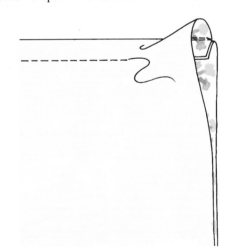

ances to just under 6mm. Turn the work to the wrong side and fold over on the seam-line. Tack and machine stitch again, just outside the enclosed seam allowances.

4 Hemming side edges

Turn under a 1.5cm wide double hem along the side edges. Press and tack in place.

5 Making the side frills

Make a 7.5cm wide strip of fabric twice the length of the blind: pin, tack and stitch strips together with narrow French

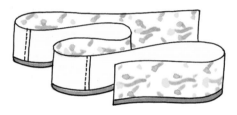

seams to the required length. Cut bias binding to the same length.

Fold bias binding evenly in half over bottom edge of frill strip, enclosing raw edges. Tack and stitch.

Run two rows of gathering stitches close together, 1.5cm from the top edge of the frill, and pull up evenly to fit the side edge of the blind.

6 Attaching frill to blind

Cut a length of bias binding the same length as the blind. Press flat then press evenly in half lengthways. Place one tacked edge of the blind over the bias binding so that the folded edge of the binding extends 5mm outside the blind. Pin and tack in position.

With right sides uppermost, position side edge of blind (with binding) over raw, gathered edge of frill. Pin, tack and

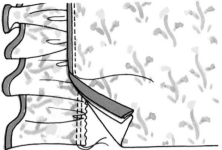

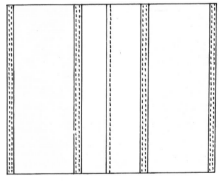

topstitch down the side edge. Repeat on the other side.

7 Positioning the vertical tapes

Mark the position of vertical tapes on the wrong side of the blind with rows of pins. Place the first two lengths at each side edge over raw edges, and the remaining tapes at equal intervals in between, about

50 to 60cm apart. Pin, tack and stitch tapes to blind, close to each tape edge in marked positions.

8 Making the heading

Turn under 1cm along the top edge of the blind and press. Position a length of curtain heading tape across the top edge of the blind, covering the raw edge of the fabric and tapes and turning under the raw ends. Knot the cord ends together at one side, leaving the cords free at the

opposite end. Pin, tack and stitch the tape in place.

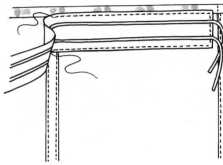

9 Making the base frill

Turn under a 1.5cm hem along the bottom edge of the blind and press. Make a 13.5cm wide strip of fabric in the same way as side frills, twice the width of the blind, plus the width of both side frills. Cut the bias binding to the same length.

Apply bias binding over the raw edge of the frill as for side frills. Run two rows of gathering stitches close together, 1.5cm from the top edge of the frill. Gather the frill evenly to fit width of blind, including side frills, continuing your line of topstitching to join the edges

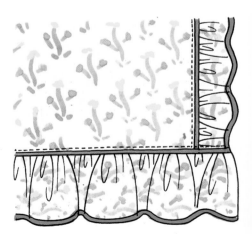

of the side frill and base frill. Neaten the side edges.

10 Attaching the rings

Stitch curtain rings, about 20cm apart, to the centre of each tape. On the centre tapes stitch the first row about 6cm above frill edge. On the side tapes, stitch the first row in line with the second row of the centre tapes. Stitch the last row on all the tapes about 30cm from the top. Make

sure that all rings align in horizontal rows.

11 Decorating the battening

Paint the battening to match the window or cover it with matching fabric. Fix the curtain track to the front of the battening.

12 Inserting lengths of cord

Pull up gathering cord evenly in the curtain heading to fit curtain track and knot together, but do not cut off. Slot curtain hooks into the heading.

Fix a picture ring screw into the base of

the battening to correspond with each vertical tape.

Cut lengths of cord, the same number as vertical tapes and each piece 2½ times the length of each vertical tape. Knot one end of the first length of cord to the left-hand bottom ring. Thread the cord up

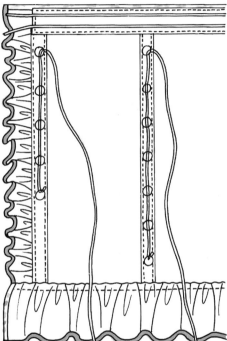

through each ring on the left-hand side tape. Do not cut off the cord.

13 Hanging the blind

Mount the blind on the curtain track, slotting the curtain hooks at each end through the end stops on the track. Thread the left-hand cord through the

A ruched blind is made like a festoon blind, but extra fullness is added to the length using gathering tape, to give a scalloped effect when the blind is down.

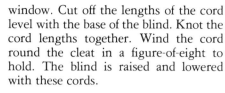

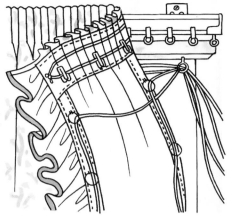

row of screw eyes in the battening. Repeat with each length of cord. Let the cords hang free at the right-hand side.

14 Gathering up and securing

Fix a cleat on to the wall at the side of the

window. Cut off the lengths of the cord level with the base of the blind. Knot the cord lengths together. Wind the cord round the cleat in a figure-of-eight to hold. The blind is raised and lowered with these cords.

Café curtains

The great advantage of café curtains is that they provide privacy and hide ugly views with a minimum loss of light. They are cheerful and welcoming, and can be made in a variety of fabrics and styles, with different headings, to suit any room.

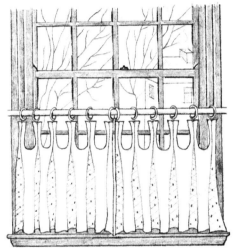

Before you begin
The kitchen is not the only suitable place for café curtains. They provide good, practical solutions to problems in other rooms too. For instance, a bedroom can be given privacy with two-tier café curtains, the bottom tier made as one and the top as a pair of curtains which can be opened and closed as required. Alternatively, a street-level sitting room can be shielded by using café curtains in a plain or sheer fabric together with full-length curtains, instead of using full-length net, which may be out of keeping

with your décor. They can also be used in place of, or in combination with, blinds made in the same fabric.

Suitable fabrics
If you plan to have a scalloped heading, the best weight of fabric is furnishing cotton, as the scallops need to stand out and keep their shape. Do not attempt to use see-through, lighter fabrics because the turnings in the facing will show through unattractively when the curtains are hung. Heavyweight materials, such as velvet, are also to be avoided, as the scalloped section would be very bulky.

Consider whether the curtains will need unusually frequent washing; if this is likely, make them with pinch pleat heading tape so that you can whip them

Small floral or geometric prints in fresh colours are best for pleated curtains.

down by slipping the hooks out of the rings when necessary.

Sheer fabrics make delightful café curtains and are particularly useful together with full-length curtains. When using sheers, use special lightweight heading tape or make a simple casing at the top and slip the curtains over a plastic-coated spring wire.

In general, small or medium-size patterns look better than large-patterned fabrics, which tend to look out of proportion.

Positioning the curtain pole
The most common position for café curtains is inside the window recess so that other curtains can be pulled over them outside the recess. However, if you are using café curtains on their own and wish to make the window look bigger, there is no reason why you should not fix the pole outside the window frame, with the brackets screwed into the wall at each side. (You may need to mount a small block of wood for the brackets so that the pole clears the window frame just enough for the curtain rings to slide along the pole.)

The position of the pole depends on the size and shape of your window: halfway down is often appropriate, but if the window is very tall, the curtains should be hung further down. Sometimes a horizontal glazing bar acts as a natural fixing point.

Calculating the amount of fabric
The style shown here gives you scallops 10cm wide and 16cm wide pleat allowances, which will be 5cm wide pleated up. To calculate the width of fabric required for a pair of curtains, measure the length of your curtain pole, divide this measurement by two and plan how many scallops and pleats will fit each curtain. Remember that café curtains

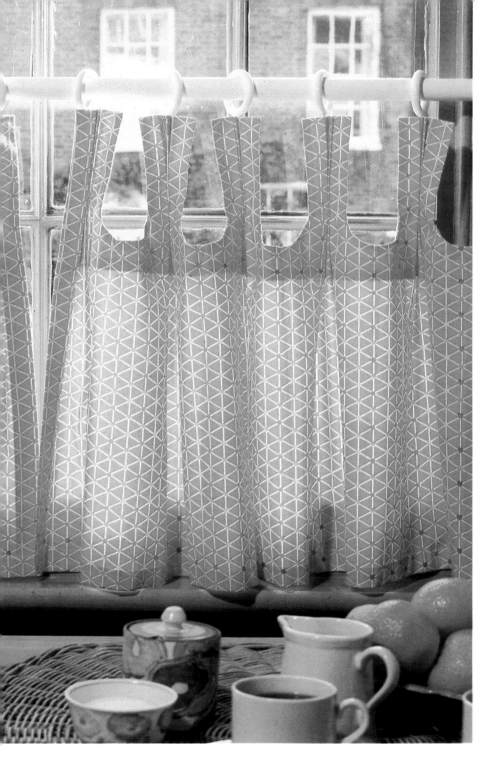

should be less gathered than ordinary curtains.

Having worked out how many scallops will fit each curtain, multiply the required number by 10cm, plus 16cm for each pleat allowance, starting and finishing with a pleat allowance. Add 5cm for each side hem.

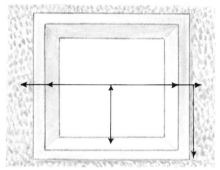

To calculate the length of fabric required, measure the distance from the curtain pole to the sill, and add 5cm for the bottom hem and 21cm for the top facing and turning. Multiply this measurement by two to get the required amount for a pair of curtains.

Materials

For a pair of café curtains for a window 120cm wide × 60 high
☐ 2.60m × 122cm wide cotton fabric
☐ Matching sewing thread
☐ 15cm × 20cm of stiff card
☐ A pair of compasses
☐ Set square
☐ Tailor's chalk

Making-up instructions

1 Making a template for the scallops

Draw a horizontal line, 10cm long, on a piece of card, and mark the centre point. Using a set square, draw a 17cm long vertical line from the centre of the base line. (The length of this line determines

the depth of the scallops and can be shortened if desired.) Using a pair of compasses, a pencil on a string or a circular object exactly 10cm in diameter, draw a circle the circumference of which touches the base line. The bottom half of

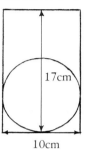

this circle forms the curved section of the scallop pattern. Draw two further vertical lines, 17cm long, one at each side of the circle; join these lines across the top. Cut out the template.

2 Joining fabric lengths

If necessary, join lengths of fabric to make up the required width, matching the pattern carefully. Press seams open.

3 Making the facing

Press a 1cm turning to the wrong side at the top edge of the fabric. Fold the top

edge to the right side of the fabric to a depth of 20cm. Tack along the top and bottom edges of the facing and press lightly, using a damp cloth.

4 Marking the scallops

Starting at the left-hand side, mark off 5cm for the side hem, then a further

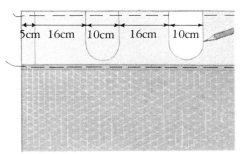

16cm for the first pleat allowance. Next, trace the outline of the first scallop, using tailor's chalk or a soft pencil. Be sure to match up the top straight edge exactly on the fold of the fabric so that the scallop is exactly vertical. Mark off the next pleat allowance, the next scallop and so on across the width of the curtain, ending with a pleat allowance and 5cm for the side hem.

5 Stitching and trimming the heading

Tack and stitch the side seams, leaving 5cm unstitched towards the bottom edge of the facing. Tack and stitch around the marked scallops. Trim away excess fabric, leaving a 1cm seam allowance, and notch the curves so that the facing will turn right side out without pucker-

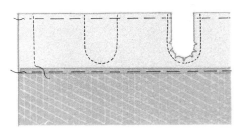

ing. Trim the side seam allowances to 1cm inside the facing to reduce bulk.

6 Finishing the scallops

Turn the scalloped heading right side out. Use the closed points of a pair of scissors to poke out the corners of the finished facing to make them neat and square. Turn under a 2.5cm wide double hem down each side; pin, tack and stitch by hand. Fold the heading back to enclose the top of each side hem and slipstitch the side opening. Stitch the base of the facing in place by hand.

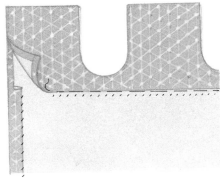

7 Making the bottom hem

Check the length carefully before turning up a 2.5cm wide double hem along the bottom. Pin, tack and stitch by hand.

8 Making the pleats

Fold the pleat allowance between each scallop into three equal pleats and stitch

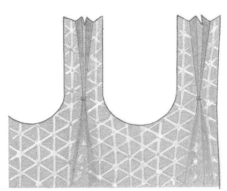

the folds together on the right side, 11cm down from the top edge.

9 Attaching rings to the pleats
Attach a ring to each group of pleats by overstitching in matching thread through the small screw head 1cm down

the back through the folds on each side of the centre pleat. Thread the rings on to the pole. If possible, position each end ring outside the bracket so that the curtains stay in position when being closed.

Café curtain headings

Café curtains can be finished in various ways to suit different windows and poles. Here are three easy alternatives, each one with a distinctive character to fit in with your individual décor.

Tabbed loops

For a window that simply needs masking, a tabbed heading on a flat café curtain is an easy arrangement to sew and very economical on fabric. Measure and cut out sufficient fabric, allowing 10cm for double hems on each side and bottom edges. Make up side hems first. Cut strips about 11.5cm wide × 23cm to make straps. Stitch down the sides, turn

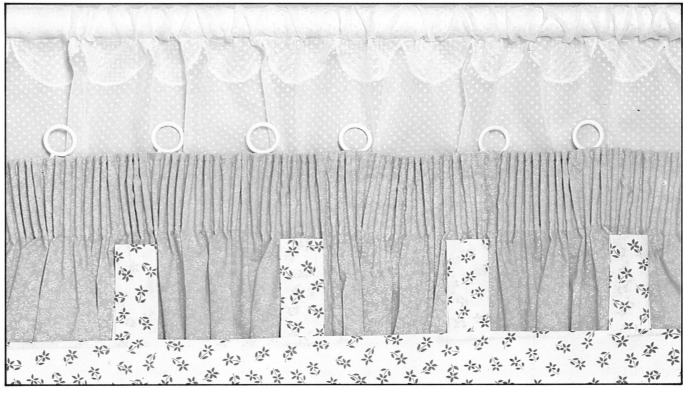

through, press and fold in half. Pin to the right side of the fabric, 1.5cm from top edge, right sides together, starting at equal distances from the corners. Cut a facing strip 11.5cm deep by the curtain width, plus 1.5cm seam allowance for sides. Place right sides together over the loops, stitch along the top edge, then fold over to the wrong side. Complete the facing hems on sides and bottom edges. Check length of curtain on the pole and then hem.

Pencil pleats

Café curtains can be made by simply using heading tape: as it will show through the window, use this method where the reverse view is not important. Measure and allow a minimum of twice the width to achieve sufficient fullness in the gathers for each curtain. Allow 2.5cm extra at the top for the heading turning, and a further 10cm for side and bottom double hems. Complete side hems first, then fold down 2.5cm at top edge; pin and tack the heading tape over the raw edge 1.5cm down from the top fold. Turn in the tape 1.5cm at each side. Machine stitch top and bottom tape edges in the same direction. Knot the ends of the cords together at one end of the tape. Pull up the cords until the curtains are the required width. Check curtain length on pole and complete bottom hem.

Scalloped casing

The scalloped casing is easy to do and economical as no special rings or poles are required. A painted dowelling rod will do. Measure the width and multiply by at least 1½ to get sufficient fullness. Add only 3cm to sides and bottom for narrow hems. Add 10cm to top edge for casing. Cut out curtains, fold double turnings, 1.5cm each down sides, and hand hem or machine stitch. Measure width and work out a circle diameter that will fit evenly spaced across the width. Trace the shape on the top edge of the fabric. Make the curve no deeper than 5cm to allow for pole casing. Cut out the shapes. Fold down casing allowance 10cm; stitch with a straight stitch 5cm down from the fold. Pin, tack and zig-zag stitch round the cut edges. Try on pole, adjust length, and complete bottom hem.

Unlined curtains

A new pair of curtains can completely transform a room. It can make a small window look bigger or a dull view brighter. Just choose a fabric that will create the right atmosphere in your home and stitch a few easy seams. If desired, add frills and ties for a pretty look.

Before you begin

Carefully consider the options before you decide on the length of your curtains; floor length will look formal and elegant, whereas sill length will look more informal and cottagey. For recessed windows you can hang the curtains from a track placed close to the frame inside the recess, or from a wider track outside the recess, above the window.

An attractive length covers the sill and hangs about 30cm below; this looks particularly effective with tie-backs.

Colourful prints, plain textured fabrics as well as lace and nets are ideal for pretty unlined curtains.

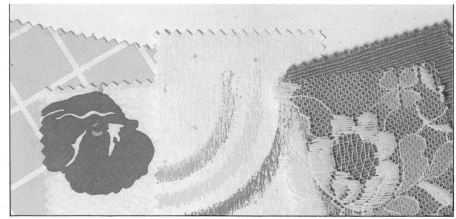

Full length curtains should not touch the floor. This will prevent them from draping well and will also make them dirty. Let them drop 2.5cm clear of the floor. For the same reasons, sill length curtains should just skim the sill.

If you have radiators in front of the windows, do not be tempted to cover them up with full length curtains. You will lose heat and could also scorch the fabric.

Fabrics

Lightweight fabrics which let the light filter through are particularly suitable for unlined curtains. Some laces have edges which form part of the pattern and do not require side hems. Cottons, cotton mixtures, lightweight synthetics, sheers and nets are good choices.

Weights

Weights are used to make the curtains hang better. There are two main types: circular weights, which are sewn into the corners, or a string of weights, enclosed in the bottom hem.

Measuring up

These instructions are for gathered curtains, using 2.5cm wide standard heading tape. There are many heading tapes available, most of which require more fabric than standard tape.

First calculate the width—always do this by measuring the curtain track. Divide this measurement by 2 if you are making a pair of curtains, and multiply this figure by 1½ to get the right fullness. Add 5cm extra for each side hem and 3cm for each join, if necessary. This will give you the total width of one curtain.

Measure the length from the curtain track to the sill or floor. To each length required, add 10cm for the bottom hem and 3.5cm at the top for the heading turnback. It is wise to allow for a certain amount of shrinkage too. Unless the fabric is guaranteed non-shrink, allow 2.5cm per 1m of fabric. This final measurement, multiplied by the number of widths (drops) required, gives you the total amount of fabric you need to buy.

Large designs

If the fabric you have chosen has a large design, you must allow extra fabric to match up. The pattern must run at the same level on every curtain. As a general rule, allow one whole extra pattern repeat per drop, except for the first drop. For example, for a pair of curtains, each with two drops, you should allow three extra pattern repeats.

Materials

The curtains shown here measure 90cm across and are 1m long. For a pair of curtains the same size without frills and ties, you will need:

☐ 2.5m × 90cm wide fabric. (If your fabric has a large pattern repeat, you will need more fabric.)
☐ 1.5m standard heading tape
☐ Matching sewing thread
☐ 2 cord tidies
☐ Weights (optional)

Making-up instructions

1 Cutting out lengths

Starting with a full pattern at the bottom (but remembering to allow for the hem), measure and cut the first length. Make sure that you start with a straight edge at the top by pulling out a single thread across the width of the fabric. Using this first piece as a guide, cut the remaining lengths, matching up the pattern.

2 Clipping the selvedges

To prevent any puckering or distortion when stitching together, clip the selvedges.

3 Joining widths

If necessary, join fabric widths. Seams should be as neat as possible, since they will show up as the light filters through your curtains. For light to medium-weight fabrics, use a French seam to join widths (see instructions on page 82). For heavier fabrics use a flat fell seam.

4 Making a flat fell seam

To make a flat fell seam, place the wrong sides together and pin, tack and stitch a 2.5cm wide seam. Trim one seam allowance down to 1cm.

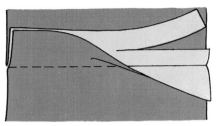

Press the seam towards the narrow edge. Fold the wide seam allowance over the trimmed edge and pin, ensuring that the fabric is lying flat.

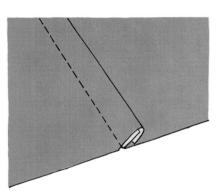

Tack and then topstitch close to the edge. Press.

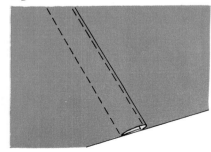

5 Matching the pattern

To join pieces of fabric with a design, first take one width and fold under the seam allowance to the wrong side along one edge. Press it flat. Place this folded edge over the seam allowance of the second width, carefully matching the pattern.

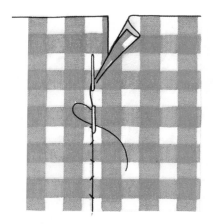

Pin and sliptack the two pieces together. To do this, pass the needle through the seam line of the bottom piece and back through the folded seam of the top piece. To stitch, turn the top piece back and with right sides now together, machine stitch along the tacked seam. Remove the sliptacking stitches.

6 Stitching the side hems

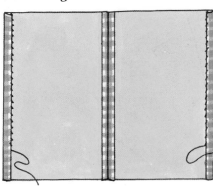

Turn under a 2.5cm double hem along each side of the curtain. Pin, tack and stitch the hem by hand or machine, leaving 50cm unstitched at the bottom edges of each side hem.

7 Positioning heading tape

Turn over and tack 3.5cm to the wrong side at the top of the curtain. Pull out 4cm of cord from both ends of the tape; knot the cord together at one end. Turn

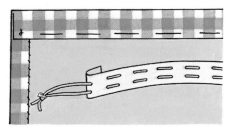

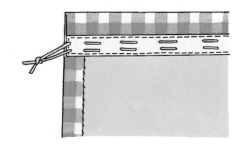

under the raw ends of the tape 1cm. Pin and tack the tape in place, overlapping the raw edge of the curtain by 1cm.

8 Stitching the heading tape

Machine stitch the heading tape close to the edges, being careful not to stitch over the cord ends.

9 Pulling up the tape

Gather up the cord so that the curtains fit across the window. Knot the ends together and wind around a cord tidy. Do not cut off the cord, or you will not be able to flatten out the curtains for

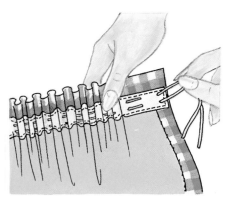

washing. Hang the curtains so that the cord tidies are at the sides of the window. Leave the curtains for two to three days before taking up the hem.

10 Marking the hem

While the curtains are still hanging, turn them up to the required length. Take them down and press the hemline. Cut off the fabric 10cm from this line.

11 Mitring the corners

Turn under a 2.5cm wide double hem at each side and press. Turn under a 5cm

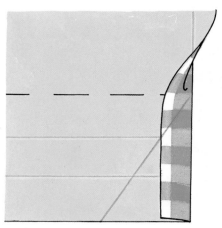

wide double hem along the bottom and press. Mark top of hem with tacking.

Unfold the side hems so a single hem remains. Unfold bottom hem completely. Fold each corner diagonally from where the tacking line meets the side edge, through the junction between the top crease and side hem, to the raw edge.

12 Turning under the side and bottom hems

Turn under the side hem again and stitch

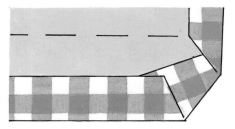

the remaining section. Turn up the bottom hem along the first fold line.

13 Stitching the bottom hem

Turn up the bottom hem once more so that it meets the side hems at the corners. If desired, slot a string of weights into the

hem or fit single weights into the corners. Stitch the hem by hand and slipstitch the folds of the mitres.

Lace is the perfect choice for light, airy curtains which provide good screening without preventing the light filtering through. A stylish finish can be achieved by draping a length of lace along the curtain pole.

Heading tapes

With the aid of the variety of heading tapes available, anyone can make beautiful, well-fitting curtains. Choose the heading, fabric and style to suit your own individual requirements.

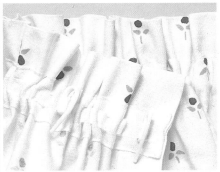

Standard tape is used for gathered curtains and requires only 1½ times the length of the curtain track. Cotton tape is suitable for all weights of fabric.

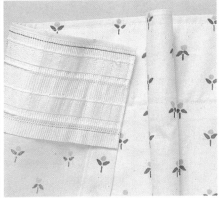

Cartridge pleating requires the same amount of fabric as pencil pleating and is suitable for all weights of fabric, sheers and nets.

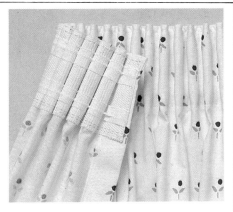

Pencil pleating tape produces crisp, immaculate pleats. It requires a fullness of 2¼ to 2½ times and is suitable for all types of fabric.

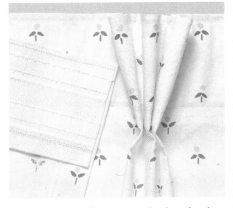

Triple pleating, or pinch pleating, requires double fullness and is suitable for all weights of fabric, sheers and nets. Extra-deep tape is available and is most suitable for floor-length curtains.

Lining tape is used for detachable lining and hooked into the heading tape of the main curtain. The same tape is used together with all types of curtain heading and it requires slightly less fullness than the main curtain.

CHAPTER 6

Dining in

The dining area is often the last place to receive full
attention when you come to decorating and soft furnishing.
But there is terrific scope for the soft touch here.

Table linen gives you no end of opportunities to emphasize or alter the décor of your dining area or kitchen. You can even change the atmosphere according to the occasion.

If your dining area is in the kitchen or living room, it is also important to give some consideration to the dining accessories. For example, it's very easy to cover a kitchen table so as to transform a useful working surface into an attractive eating area, or dress up a side table in a living room and move it to the centre of the room to serve as a dining table.

Don't forget that it's not just the table linen which furnishes the dining area, but also curtains and cushions, which give scope for adapting the style and colour scheme of your room to suit your needs. And tablecloths need not be limited to the dining room—circular tables have become a standard feature of interior design in many rooms in the home.

Colours and styles

As well as creating a pleasant atmosphere, soft furnishings in the dining room should complement your china and the meals you are serving. Choose your first set of china with flexibility in mind. For example, simple blue and white china can look equally good in formal or informal settings. A pretty, pastel pink cloth in fine fabric dresses the china up for special occasions, while a natural, rough-woven linen or blue check fabric is more serviceable for everyday use. At breakfast or tea-time, gentle, floral chintzes bring a cottagey look to your table.

If you collect more than one set of china, your choice of style will widen, and you can introduce even more colours and looks to your table. If you are building up a range of table linen, it may be advisable to keep other furnishings in the room simple. Do ensure that your

Table linen looks lovely embellished with embroidery or cutwork.

table linen matches the other furnishings as well as the china.

Because of the different elements of table linen (cloth, napkins, table mats, napkin rings, even egg and tea cosies) you have great scope for mixing and matching patterned and plain fabrics. When using co-ordinating fabrics to make a show, ensure that the table mat stands out from the cloth, to define the place setting. Any binding round the edge of the mat is best done using a colour which contrasts with both the tablecloth and the mat.

Some of the smaller items of table linen give you the opportunity to develop specialized sewing skills. Table mats are more useful if they are quilted; napkin rings can be shaped and scalloped; and there are endless opportunities for embroidery and appliqué. Why not decorate a plain cloth to match your best set of china for a special touch?

If you sew your own table linen you can also add personal touches by making lined baskets to hold bread and rolls, or carefully designed, thick mats that are just the right size for your casseroles and serving dishes.

There is great scope for co-ordinating table linen with other furnishings. Make a light, throw-over lace cloth with a darker cloth underneath, matching the lace to net curtains at the windows. With plain curtains, make tie-backs in remnants of the cotton fabric you use for napkins. You can make bread basket liners to match chair cushions. The possibilities are endless.

Practicalities

Whatever your fantasy dining room is like, it must be practical. If table mats are to be useful as well as attractive, they must insulate against heat penetrating from dishes through to the table. You can place cork mats under fabric mats or cloths, but it is more practical to incorporate insulation into the mats. One way to do this is with Milium, a metallized fabric which reflects heat and can be sewn into a quilted mat. This fabric can also be used to make insulating gloves to use when you bring hot dishes to the table.

Whatever your choice of fabric, it is essential that it is easily washable. And if it has minimum-iron qualities as well, like cotton/polyester or seersucker, so much the better. It's a good idea to be sure you have the time and patience to care for table linen before you embark on a project. There's no point in carefully

Left and right: Hand-sewn place mats and napkins decorated with fine lawn appliqué and embroidery bring a touch of elegance to the dinner table.

hand-rolling hems on a beautiful damask cloth and saving money by sewing linen yourself if you are going to have to spend a fortune on sending it to the laundry for a proper launder, starch and press.

If cloths are kept in place permanently, make sure they are in a suitable fabric. A patterned or plain PVC cloth, for example, makes a practical cover for a table in a breakfast room, as it protects the table and is easy to wipe clean.

When a good table has to double as a workspace, for hobbies or homework for example, protect the surface with a heavy-duty quilted cloth so that there is no danger of marking the surface with ink or biro, scratching it or causing white heat rings from mugs of tea or coffee.

The designer table

A popular furnishing element in any room—as a side table in the dining room, as an occasional table and focal point in the sitting room, or as a bedside table in the bedroom—is the circular table or 'designer table', dressed up with a lavish cloth.

The table itself does not have to be well finished. A simple chipboard framework is adequate, as the whole table is covered by a floor-length cloth. And there is no reason why you should not add extra layers of cloths just for effect. For example, start with a plain, circular cloth, add a plain or patterned square cloth to give a 'handkerchief hem' effect, and top it off with a circular lace cloth.

The possibilities are endless and, like the changing styles of table linen described earlier, a quick change of tablecloth on a designer table can change the emphasis of colour and style in a room.

Here a square tablecloth is used over a circular one. The lace trim makes a feature of the corners, and the embroidery enhances any centrepiece.

Stylish table settings

Add a fresh look to your dining table with a new set of matching place mats, coasters and napkins. Cotton fabrics offer a wide choice of colours and prints to complement your china, and to be really practical the mats are reversible. A darker square check has been used on one side for practical everyday use and a pretty toning print on the reverse for a more romantic occasion.

The mats are made with a layer of wadding inserted between the two sides of fabric, which are quilted together quite simply by machine stitching along the lines of the check fabric (or along tacked quilting lines if it's not checked). To complete the set, add alternative napkins to match either side of the mats.

Before you begin

The most suitable fabrics are fairly firm cottons with sufficient body to make the napkins reasonably crisp. The firmness is also good for the mats, as the fabric will be less likely to stretch or become distorted when being quilted. Ensure that your fabrics, wadding and binding are all washable.

The quilting may be worked in a contrasting colour, which will show up smartly, but it will also highlight any unevenness in the stitching. It is often easier to achieve a professional finish by using a thread to match the background colour of the fabric so that a little unevenness in the stitching will not be quite so noticeable.

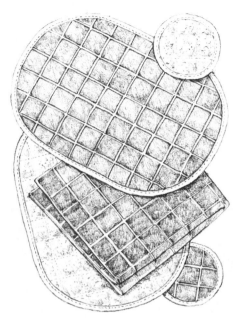

Choose crisp cottons in matching, contrasting or reversible designs.

96

When cutting out the mats, make sure that the straight edges of the mats are parallel to the selvedges of the fabric so that the quilting lines can follow the grain of fabric.

Materials

For four place mats and coasters
- ☐ 50cm × 120cm wide floral fabric
- ☐ 50cm × 120cm wide check fabric
- ☐ 50cm × 90cm wide wadding
- ☐ Matching sewing thread

For four napkins
- ☐ 1m × 120cm wide fabric
- ☐ Matching sewing thread

Making the place mats and coasters

Cutting out

Following the fabric cutting layout, cut out four mats 35cm × 25cm and four coasters 12cm square from each fabric. Cut each piece once from wadding as shown in the wadding cutting layout. Press the fabric pieces well.

If you are not using a check fabric, mark out the quilting lines 3.5cm apart and parallel to the edges; mark with tacking lines or very lightly with tailor's chalk on one set of fabric pieces.

Cutting layout for fabric

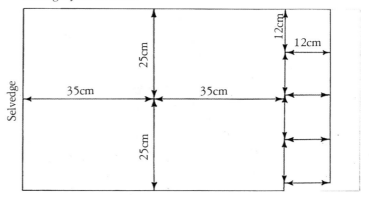

Cutting layout for wadding

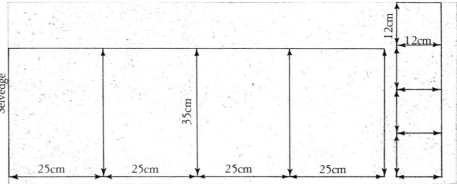

2 Tacking the pieces together

With the right sides outwards, sandwich the wadding between the two contrasting

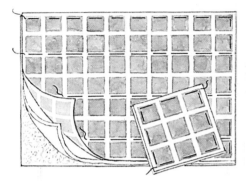

fabric pieces. Pin and tack around the edges and across the width of the mats at about 7cm intervals along the quilting lines.

3 Quilting the mats

Quilt the three layers together using a medium-length machine stitch. Follow-

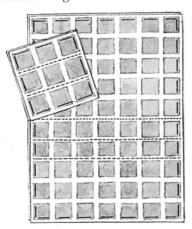

ing the lines of the fabric check (or quilting lines), stitch all the shorter lines first, working from the centre line out to each side. Always start stitching at the same edge of fabric.

4 Finishing quilting

Remove central rows of tacking. Complete quilting by stitching the

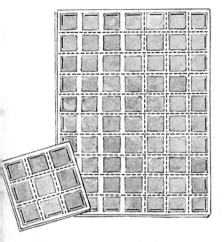

second set of lines at right angles to the first. Again start each row at the same edge.

5 Trimming mats to shape

Using a saucer, round off the corners of the mats. Trim corners and edges evenly.

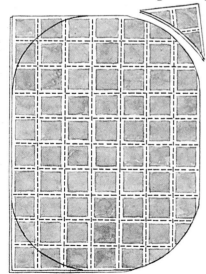

Using a small bowl, redraw coasters to a circular shape and trim.

6 Preparing the binding

Cut bias binding to fit the edges of the table mats and coasters, allowing for ends to be joined along the straight grain.

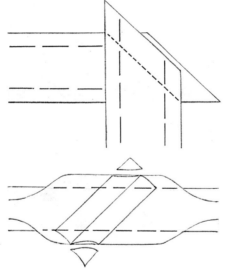

Unfold the binding at the ends and join together in the same way as bias strips are joined; make sure binding is not twisted before joining. Press seams open, fold and re-press binding as it was before. Fold binding in half lengthways with upper folded half a little narrower than the under half.

7 Attaching the binding

With the narrower half uppermost, insert the edge of the mat into the binding. If

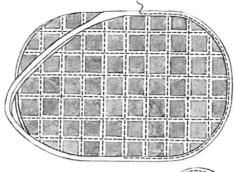

you have difficulty inserting the quilted edge of the mats into the binding, machine stitch around the edge of mats after trimming them to shape and before inserting edge into binding. Pin and tack in place through all thicknesses. Topstitch binding in place, and press binding only.

Making the napkins

1 Cutting out

Cut out four napkins approximately 50cm square; 1cm hems are allowed.

2 Hemming the edges

Press 5mm, then another 5mm to the wrong side along two opposite edges of the napkins. Machine stitch in place.

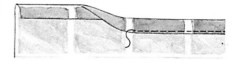

In the same way press and stitch narrow hems along the remaining two opposite edges of napkins.

Contrast binding on these napkins and quilted placemats not only makes them into a set but also matches the china.

Matching table linen

Brighten up meal times with this smart set, a pretty patterned tablecloth and napkin rings with scallop-edged napkins to match. And for bread rolls or fruit, line a basket in a matching patterned fabric.

Before you begin
Use easy-care fabrics for your table set. The fabrics must wash well at high temperatures, as meal-time stains can be hard to remove, so choose cotton, cotton

mixtures or linens. For a really chic look, mix patterned and plain fabrics together, and add toning or contrasting stitching to highlight the edges. If you have a very large table to cover, pick cotton sheeting, which comes in extra wide widths, and is available with patterns as well as plain—it looks just as good out of the bedroom.

Calculating the amounts

The tablecloth
Measure the table top and add a generous allowance on all sides for the overhang— at least 25cm–30cm for an attractive length. Add 1cm all round for the hem.

If it is necessary to join widths of fabric to gain the correct size, position the seams at the sides of the table rather than centrally so that they are as unobtrusive as possible.

The lined basket
Measure the length and width of the base and add 1.5cm all round. Measure round the sides of the basket at the top and add half as much again. Measure the depth of the basket and add 6cm. You will need enough fabric for these two sections, plus lightweight wadding for the base.

Plain fabrics, pretty florals or fresh modern designs are good choices for this table linen.

Making the tablecloth

Materials
For a cloth 100cm × 100cm
- [ ] 1.10m × 122cm wide fabric
- [ ] Matching sewing thread

1 Cutting out
Trim the fabric to 102cm square.

2 Making the hem
Turn under a 5mm wide double hem all round the cloth, mitring the corners.

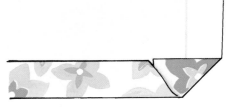

Pin, tack and stitch by machine close to the edge all round, using matching sewing thread.

Making the napkins

Materials
For a set of four napkins 45cm square
- [ ] 1m × 122cm wide plain fabric
- [ ] Contrasting sewing thread

1 Making the pattern
Cut a piece of paper 45cm square. Fold

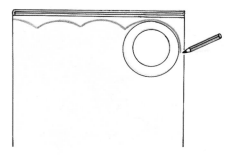

the paper in half, and then in half again widthways. Using a round cup, tin or bottle as a template, mark half a scallop at the side corners diagonally opposite each other, two scallops along each side and one scallop round the remaining corner. Cut out round the scalloped edge. Unfold the paper and check the pattern.

2 Cutting out the fabric
Using the pattern, cut out four napkins from plain fabric.

3 Stitching the scallops
Set the sewing machine to a close, fairly wide zig-zag stitch. Using contrasting thread, stitch round the edges of each

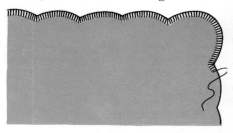

napkin. Thread the ends neatly into the stitching to finish.

Making the napkin rings

Materials
For a set of four napkin rings 3cm wide and 15cm long
- [ ] 10cm × 122cm wide printed fabric
- [ ] Scrap of iron-on interfacing
- [ ] Contrasting sewing thread

1 Cutting out
From printed fabric cut out two pieces 17.5cm × 4cm for each napkin ring. Cut out four pieces the same size from iron-on interfacing.

2 Joining the pieces
For each napkin ring fuse the interfacing

to the wrong side of one fabric piece. Place the second piece on the interfaced side of the first piece, wrong sides inwards; pin and tack together.

3 Making the pattern

Cut a piece of paper 1.5 × 3cm. Using a round template, mark five scallops centrally along both sides of the paper,

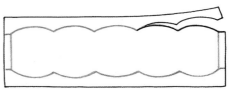

leaving 1cm straight at each end. Cut around the scalloped edge.

4 Stitching the rings

Position the pattern centrally over the fabric strip and pin in place. With a pencil, trace the outline of the pattern. Remove the pattern and stitch round the scalloped outline, leaving 1cm free at each end. Pin and stitch the short edges of the interfaced fabric together to form a

ring. Trim seam allowances and open out seam. Trim the remaining edges and tuck in; slipstitch the opening to close.

5 Finishing the scallops

Cut round the napkin rings, just outside the stitched lines. Set the sewing machine to a close zig-zag stitch. Using contrasting thread, stitch round each side. Finish off ends neatly.

Making the lined basket

Materials
☐ Oval basket 23cm × 22cm, 8cm deep
☐ 30cm × 122cm wide printed fabric
☐ Scrap of lightweight wadding
☐ 20cm × 50cm plain fabric
☐ Matching sewing thread

1 Cutting out
Cut out one piece of fabric and one piece of wadding for the base, plus one strip of fabric for the sides.

2 Quilting the base
Place the wadding on the wrong side of the fabric, edges matching, and tack together.

3 Making the side strip
Pin, tack and stitch the fabric strip together along the short sides, taking a

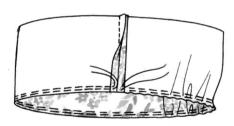

1.5cm seam allowance, to form a ring. Run a double line of gathering stitches round one long edge and pull up the gathers to fit round the base.

4 Joining the base and side strip
With right sides together, pin the gathered edge of the strip to the base, spacing the gathers evenly to fit. Pin, tack and stitch in place 1.5cm from the raw edges.

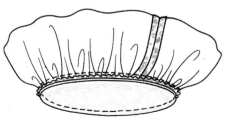

5 Making slits for the handles
Position the lining inside the basket and

mark where the handles fall. Cut 5cm slits to accommodate each side of them. Make up about 50cm of bias binding from plain fabric and fold it evenly in half

over raw edges of each slit. Pin, tack and stitch in place.

6 Making the casing and ties
Turn under 1cm and then 1.5cm at the top edge to form a narrow casing. Pin, tack and stitch. Make up 1m of rouleau from plain fabric and thread it through the casing. Place the lining inside the basket and over the top edge. Pull up rouleau and tie a bow round one handle.

Circular tablecloths

A set of co-ordinating tablecloths in fresh, modern fabrics will brighten up your décor and give an old table a new lease of life. Here a floor-length frilled cloth has been covered with a short circular cloth in a pretty floral print. Both cloths are edged with bias binding.

Before you begin

A circular cloth requires a simple pattern and, unless your table is very small, lengths of fabric will have to be joined. The joins should be made at each side of the cloth.

A short cloth can be made from a plain circle of fabric with the overhang 30cm–40cm long; this type of cloth is particularly suitable for a dining table. A floor-length cloth can be made either in the same way, or from a central panel that fits the table top with a floor-length gathered frill or skirt. This is more suitable for a side table or as a decorative design feature in a room, but less practical for everyday use. It may be used with a smaller cloth in toning or contrasting fabric placed over the top of the gathered cloth.

Suitable fabrics

Cotton and linen are good, hardwearing fabrics, which hang well and have the crisp finish required for a decorative and lasting tablecloth.

When considering day-to-day care and laundering, a synthetic fabric or a mixture, such as cotton/polyester, is

Plain fabric, gingham and small printed patterns are good choices; avoid large one-way designs.

more practical. If a synthetic fabric is used, it must be of reasonable weight to hang well.

Plain or patterned fabrics are equally suitable, and a combination of both can be used for a set of two cloths. If a patterned fabric is used for a frilled cloth, make sure that it can be used sideways, as the width of the fabric will be the depth of the frill.

Do not choose a large design if your table is small—as a general rule, match the scale of the pattern to the size of the table for which the cloth is intended.

If desired, plain fabric can be decorated with, for example, appliqué or embroidery.

Edgings

Various edgings may be used to finish the cloth in a decorative way. The simplest is to bind the raw edge with bias binding, or to add a fringe or braid.

A short gathered frill will look attractive on the edge of a cloth; make it twice the circumference.

A scalloped edge looks very pretty: a round template is used for tracing the scallops on to the fabric, and the outline is machine stitched with a close zig-zag. The surplus fabric is trimmed away close to the stitching.

Appliqué looks effective round the edge of a short cloth, particularly with the motif repeated in the centre.

Making a plain circular tablecloth

Calculating the amount of fabric

Measure the diameter of the table, then decide how much overhang you want.

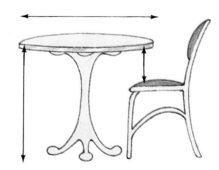

For a short cloth, measure from the top of the table to a chair seat; for a long cloth, measure to the floor. Multiply the over-

hang by two and add to the diameter of the table. This will give you the diameter of the finished tablecloth.

If the diameter is less than the width of your selected fabric, one length of fabric is sufficient. However, if the diameter is wider, you will need to join two or more lengths of fabric. If the fabric has a large design, also allow one extra pattern repeat per extra length of fabric for matching.

Materials

For a tablecloth 2m in diameter
- ☐ 4m × 122cm wide fabric (if the fabric has a large design, add one extra pattern repeat)
- ☐ 6.5m bias binding for edging (or 50cm plain fabric)
- ☐ Matching sewing thread
- ☐ Paper for pattern
- ☐ A piece of string and a pencil

1 Joining lengths of fabric

Starting with a straight edge, cut one length of fabric, the same length as the diameter of the finished cloth. Cut the remaining fabric in half lengthways. Join one strip to each side of the first length,

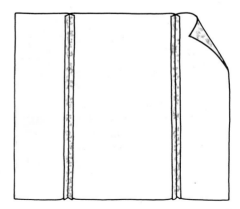

taking a 1.5cm wide seam allowance and taking care to match the pattern; pin, sliptack and machine stitch together (see

step 4 on page 90). Cut the strips level with the first length of fabric. Trim seam allowances to 1cm; neaten the raw edges.

2 Marking the centre of the cloth

Fold the fabric in half, right sides together, and fold it in half again. Mark

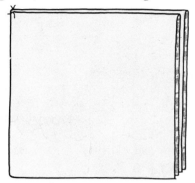

the corner which is the centre of the fabric with a tailor's tack.

3 Making the pattern

Cut a square of paper, the same size as the folded fabric. Take a piece of string and tie one end round a pin and the other end around a pencil; the distance between the

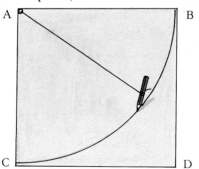

pin and the pencil should equal the radius of the tablecloth. Put the pin at corner A of the paper square and, holding the pen at right angles to the paper, draw an arc from B to C. Cut out the pattern.

4 Cutting out the fabric

Place the pattern on the folded fabric so that corner A is on top of the tailor's

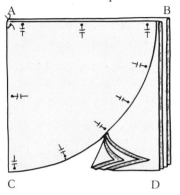

tack. Pin and cut out along the curved line of the pattern from C to B.

5 Cutting bias strips

If you are making your own bias binding, cut out the strips along the bias. To find the bias grain, fold the fabric so that one

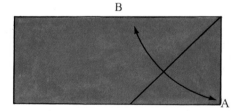

selvedge is at right angles to the other selvedge (from A to B).

Cut along the fold line and cut 2.5cm

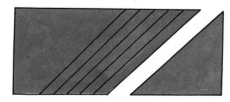

wide strips which are parallel to the first cutting line.

6 Joining strips

Place the strips with right sides together and raw edges matching. Pin, tack and machine stitch 1cm from the edge.

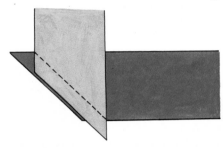

Unfold the strip, press the seam open and trim the corners.

7 Folding the binding

Turn under 5mm to the wrong side of the fabric along each edge and press well.

8 Applying binding

Remove the pattern and then unfold the fabric.

Unfold one edge of the binding and place it along the raw edge of the fabric,

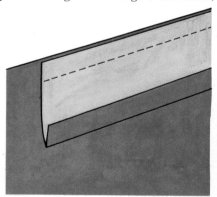

with right sides together and with raw edges matching.

Pin in position. Tack and machine stitch along the fold line.

Fold the binding over to the wrong side

of the fabric. Slipstitch by hand along the original seamline, or machine stitch 2mm from the edge.

Making a floor-length cloth with gathered frill

Calculating the amount of fabric

Measure the diameter of the table. Add 2cm to this measurement for seam allowances. This is the diameter of the top piece and equals the length of fabric required. However, if your table is wider than the fabric, you will need two lengths plus one extra pattern repeat for matching the design.

Measure the distance from the table top to the floor and add 1cm for the seam allowance. This is the total depth of the frill and it should be cut from the width of the fabric.

To calculate the length of fabric required for the frill, measure the circumference of the table. For a fairly full frill, allow twice this measurement. If less fullness is required, 1½ times is sufficient. Also add 3cm for seam allowances. This measurement will also give you the required length of bias binding for the bottom edge.

Materials

For a tablecloth 120cm in diameter with a full, 75cm deep frill
- ☐ 10.5m × 122cm wide fabric
- ☐ 9.25m bias binding for edging (or 50cm plain fabric)
- ☐ Matching sewing thread
- ☐ Paper for pattern

1 Cutting out the fabric

Cut out the circular piece for the tablecloth as for the short cloth. (Unless your table is wider than 120cm, you will not need to join lengths of fabric.) Cut the length of the frill, then cut along one side of the fabric to get the correct depth.

2 Making the frill

With right sides together, pin, tack and machine stitch the short sides of the frill, taking a 1.5cm wide seam allowance. Neaten the raw edges and press the seam open.

Using the longest stitch length on your sewing machine, make a double row of stitching 1cm from the top edge of the frill.

At the ends of these gathering lines, wind the threads round a pin in a figure-of-eight to make it easier to adjust the gathers.

Carefully pull up the bobbin threads of the two gathering rows until the frill is the right size.

3 Stitching the frill to the top piece

With right sides together and raw edges matching, pin the frill to the top piece, making sure that the gathers are evenly spaced. Tack carefully and machine stitch 1cm from the edge. Remove the tacking thread and press the seam allowances towards the top piece; trim and neaten raw edges. Finish the edge of the frill with bias binding as instructed for the short cloth.

CHAPTER 7

Personal touches

However well designed the soft furnishings are in your home,
it is the little extras which add the important details that
make all the difference.

ny interior designer can come up with an effective scheme for a room, but the skilled designer will also incorporate little collections of accessories: a set of ceramic dishes on the mantelpiece, a group of picture frames on the dressing table. There is no reason why many of these finishing touches should not be hand-made. Small projects give you an opportunity to use up remnants of fabrics used elsewhere in the room.

This is also an ideal way to experiment with new techniques and develop new skills. Padded, embroidered or appliquéed picture frames, for example, are both useful and decorative, but not too daunting for the inexperienced home sewer. And if you are developing your own ideas and working out new designs, it will not be a total disaster if your plans fail. With only small amounts of fabric involved, you can discard any mishaps and start again.

Some small projects also give you the opportunity of working with more extravagant fabrics. Little scraps of silk make an appliqué design special. You can also experiment with other techniques, like painting fabric.

We give three project ideas here, but there are many, many more ideas which help to add the soft touch.

Storage ideas

It is often very practical to use fabric bags and pockets to store items. The traditional peg bag—a large pocket hanging from a coat hanger—is convenient and can be made to look very attractive. In the dining room, sets of good cutlery can be stored in green baize pockets so they are protected against scratching.

In the living room, unsightly sewing clutter can be stored away in pretty lined baskets, while in the bathroom or bedroom the same type of basket can be

used for make-up and trinkets. A jewellery roll—a quilted panel with pockets for necklaces, earrings and bangles, which rolls up compactly—will protect valuables when you travel, and on the same principle you can store a portable sewing kit.

In the bedroom, you can make use of the back of the door or the inside of a wardrobe door by making a set of hanging pockets in which to store shoes. A matching stocking tidy, like the one on page 114, adds an even more personal touch.

The hanging pocket idea can be adapted for other purposes too. In a child's room, make it in bright colours and adapt the shapes of the pockets to suit specific needs: sports equipment, books and stationery, collections of semi-precious stones or shells. The pockets can even be made from clear plastic to show off a collection.

Display ideas

An instant way to add a personal touch to a room is to display a collection of family photographs. Sepia or old black and white pictures look delightful in Victorian silver and wooden frames, with colour pictures in more modern, simple steel or perspex frames. And there is no reason why a favourite picture should not be set into a fabric frame. The simplest frames can be made from fabric-covered card. The delightful painted and padded frame on page 110 is rather more elaborate, and so has been used for a mirror rather than a picture. If used as a picture frame, the frame and picture could easily detract from each other, with the overall effect being lost.

Another display idea using fabric is to make a noticeboard. Traditional green baize or felt is easy to work with, but there are many refinements. The basis of a noticeboard is a piece of softboard or insulation board, covered in fabric. Add a criss cross of tapes, so that you can slip bills and mail in behind them until you have time to deal with them. Add a set of hanging pockets, like those described earlier, to hold stationery for a home—office noticeboard.

Noticeboards are more effective if they are screwed firmly to the wall, rather than free hanging.

Fun ideas

It's always nice to be a bit adventurous in some projects. If you are reasonably handy with the sewing machine, you will be able to apply your knowledge to making soft sculptures—a development of a simple cushion, for instance, or shapes that are really toys and will keep children amused for hours.

Babies love to see movement, and a mobile is a cheerful addition to the nursery. A very effective and easy theme to try is a sun with raindrops and a rainbow—but there are many other themes you could develop: animals, birds, or just simple geometric shapes in bright colours.

You can use remnants of fabric for many other fun ideas in children's rooms. Make large felt appliqué pictures to decorate walls, or big, floppy toys to cuddle. Pyjama cases are always popular. They needn't necessarily be in the shape of animals—try cars, aeroplanes, or jolly pot plant shapes. Bean bags in the shape of frogs will provide hours of entertainment for both young and old: they can take on extraordinarily life-like postures.

Useful ideas

There are many other ways in which fabric can usefully be put to work around the home. Drawstring bags in all shapes and sizes have unlimited uses. A huge bag, hung on the back of the bathroom door, or on each individual bedroom door, keeps clothes out of the way until washday. On a smaller scale, a drawstring bag can be used as a shoebag to protect shoes in a suitcase, or as a washbag if it is lined with waterproof fabric.

In the kitchen, you can make oven mitts and gloves in cheerful colours to match your décor. And if an unsightly food mixer has to be stored on the worksurface, why not make a cover in quilted or PVC fabric? It will stop dust and grease collecting on the machine as well as keeping it out of sight.

There are many useful fabric touches you can add to the nursery. A dual-purpose changing mat and bag, with a padded waterproof surface and pockets for talc, cream, nappies and so on, is indispensable for the baby on the move. And at bathtime a towelling wrap with a

Far left: Dress up a round table with a circular frilled cloth, topped by a square cloth with the centre of each edge pleated up to the rim of the table, and trimmed with ribbon. Left: A matching set of hanging tidy, mirror frame, tissue box cover and lined basket adds charm to a bathroom. Right: Make a beautiful photo album cover and frame from moiré taffeta, trimmed with lace and plaited satin ribbon.

fitted hood will keep baby warm as well as dry.

Fabric choice

Before embarking on a project, consider your materials carefully. Choose fabrics of a suitable weight and style for the task in hand. Tough, brightly patterned cotton is ideal for a laundry bag, for instance, while a shoe bag should be made in a softer fabric—you could even make one out of a soft duster.

The fabric should also fit in with the décor of the room. In a child's room a set of hanging pockets on the back of the door in bright cotton canvas adds a splash of colour. In a more softly decorated room, a similar set of pockets can be made to melt into the background by using the same fabric as the curtains or bedspread, or a plain fabric in the same colour as the door on which it hangs.

The ranges of co-ordinated fabrics and wallcoverings now in the shops give great scope for adding personal touches. Mix and match accessories in different colourways of the same geometric design, or use different patterns in toning colours. Indeed it is often the mixing together of toning colours and designs which is the main attraction of the latest ranges of wall-coverings and fabrics.

Collect all your remnants of fabric and keep them neatly ordered, according to type (velvet, cotton, etc) and colour. Then when you're feeling inspired, with a little time on your hands, you can raid the rag bag and create your own very personal finishing touches.

Bluebell mirror frame

This exquisite mirror frame with its delightful bluebell appliqué design is made from pure silks. Acrylic paints have been used to enhance the design and add interesting detail.

Before you begin

Silks are ideal to work with because of the vividness of the colours and the very fine weave of the fabric which minimizes fraying. You will need about six different shades of blue and five different shades of green, plus a mauve and a bluish purple to produce a varied colour scheme. Here, a pure silk dupion has been used for the background.

In addition to silk fabrics, you will need some acrylic paints in blues, greens and mauve in order to complete the design.

The mirror can be obtained from a glazier. It is advisable to tape the sharp edges with masking tape to prevent accidents. A piece of hardboard, a piece of stiff card and a piece of wadding the same size as the mirror, are required. The hardboard is used to back the mirror, and the card and wadding form the frame upon which the silk fabric is mounted. A piece of cartridge paper is placed at the back of the hardboard to cover the raw edges of the silk.

Materials

For a mirror frame, 32cm × 40cm
- 50cm × 90cm wide cream silk dupion
- Scraps of very thin silk fabrics in blues, greens, mauve and purple
- 40cm × 32cm of medium-weight wadding
- Paper-backed bonding
- Mirror, 40cm × 32cm
- Thick white card, 40cm × 32cm
- Hardboard, 40cm × 32cm
- PVA adhesive
- Masking tape
- Double-sided adhesive tape
- Artist's acrylic paints in blues, greens and mauve
- Watercolour brushes
- Cartridge paper, 38cm × 30cm
- Dressmaker's graph paper
- Two eyelet screws

Making-up instructions

1 Enlarging the design
Using dressmaker's graph paper, enlarge the design on page 112 to the right size.

2 Preparing the background
Using pattern, cut out the silk dupion adding 8cm all round to allow for turnings (56cm × 48cm). Paint the lower area, up to the base of the bluebell leaves, with pale green paint. When this has dried, paint little tufts of grass all over this area using a very fine brush.

3 Cutting out the hardboard and card frame
Place the mirror on the smooth side of the hardboard and trace the outline. Using a saw and following the outline exactly, cut out. Smooth the edges with glasspaper, if necessary. Trace the outline of the mirror on the thick white card and cut out, using a sharp craft knife. Transfer the inner edges of the pattern on to the card and very carefully cut out the window piece with the craft knife. Stick a layer of masking tape all round the edges of the mirror to cover the sharp edges of the glass.

Alternative colour schemes may be chosen and the position of the flowers and leaves varied to give an individual interpretation of the design.

4 Mounting the background silk on the card frame
Transfer the flower design on to the card frame. Lay the silk on the frame, right sides uppermost, with the silk extending 8cm outside the frame all round. Cut out the window shape from the fabric, leaving 3cm all round to allow for turnings. Apply a small amount of adhesive to the protruding card shapes and stick the fabric in position; leave to dry. Turn the card over and fold the

edges of the raw silk in the window area to the back. Apply adhesive to the card, pull the fabric edges tight and stick down

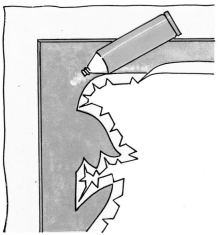

to the back of the card, snipping in to the fabric round curves and at corners to make it lie flat.

5 Cutting out flowers and leaves
Trace off several leaf and flower shapes on to the paper backed-bonding. Cut out roughly round each shape and iron on to the wrong side of the appropriately coloured silk. Cut out the shapes carefully with sharp scissors.

111

6 Laying out the design

Following the design seen through the silk background, lay out the silk flower and leaf shapes, overlapping where necessary. Draw out some long random leaf shapes for the bluebells. Reverse these drawings, and, using the same method as before, cut out these shapes having backed them with the bonding. When you are satisfied with the design, peel off the backing paper on each piece and iron it in place on the silk dupion, following the manufacturer's instructions. Where the motifs overlap, start with the bottom pieces and build up the design gradually.

Each square = 2cm

7 Painting the details

Iron the whole piece of silk flat, and, using the traced design as a guide, paint in the stems and extra leaves in green.

Paint shading on the flowers in various blues and purples. Using a very fine brush, paint the veins on the violet leaves. Make the painting go beyond the outer edges of the card to go round the edges of the frame.

8 Padding the frame

Cut out a piece of wadding exactly the

size of the card frame, omitting the protruding shapes around the window. Sandwich the wadding between the card and the background silk. Stick it down on the

card using double-sided adhesive tape. Smooth the silk over the padding.

9 Framing the mirror

Using double-sided adhesive tape, stick the hardboard on to the wrong side of the mirror, and then the mirror on to the wrong side of the padded card. Make sure all the edges are level. Place the mirror face down on a clean, flat surface and pull the surplus silk to the back all round the

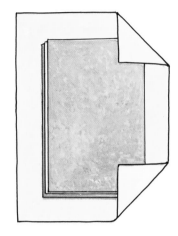

edges. Starting with the corners, glue the extra silk to the hardboard backing using PVA adhesive. Pull the silk taut along each edge in turn and glue in place. To make the padding even, press down the mirror with your left hand as you pull the silk. Leave to dry.

10 Finishing the back

Cut out a piece of cartridge paper to 30cm × 38cm. Glue this to the back of the mirror frame to cover the raw edges of the fabric. Screw two eyelet screws in to the back of the mirror for hanging.

This padded satin mirror frame is made in much the same way, but it features embroidery with the appliqué, and the inner edge is piped.

Wardrobe accessories

Keep your wardrobe tidy and your shoes neatly tucked away in this stylish shoe tidy made from co-ordinating fabrics. The additional stocking tidy may be hung below the shoes or rolled up and kept in a drawer. The stocking tidy is also ideal for travelling and holidays as it easily packs into a suitcase.

Before you begin

To be practical, choose a closely woven, washable fabric such as a firm cotton. The shoe tidy is suspended from a length of wooden dowelling slotted through a casing at the top edge. When laundering, simply remove the dowelling and replace it afterwards.

The tidies may be hung on the inside of a wardrobe door or on the bedroom door. Either way they will make an attractive addition especially if you use fabrics which harmonize with your bedroom colour scheme.

To minimize the need for laundering, use a darker fabric for the inside of the shoe tidy and the same fabric to line the pockets so that any marks rubbing off the shoes are less likely to show. Make the outer side of the pockets in a co-ordinating fabric in a lighter colour and also use this fabric to back the tidy so as to give an attractive contrasting finish along the top edge. If desired, two ribbon ties attached to the lower edge of the shoe tidy can be threaded through two loops at the top of the stocking tidy to hang it in place.

For the stocking tidy, use the pretty lighter fabric for the pockets and the inside, and the practical darker fabric for the outside.

Materials

☐ 1.50m × 120cm wide dark fabric
☐ 1.80m × 120cm wide light fabric
☐ 11.50m × 12mm wide bias binding
☐ Matching sewing thread
☐ 3m × 6mm wide ribbon
☐ 54cm × 12mm diameter dowelling
☐ Paint for ends of dowelling

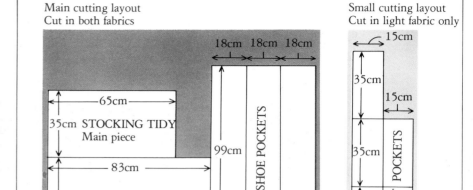

Main cutting layout
Cut in both fabrics

Small cutting layout
Cut in light fabric only

Making the shoe tidy

1 Cutting out

Mark out the pieces on to a single layer of the appropriate fabric as shown in the cutting layout. From darker fabric, cut out the pieces on the main layout. From the lighter fabric, cut out the pieces on the main layout and also those on the small layout.

2 Binding shoe pockets

With wrong sides facing, place one dark

pocket strip on each light pocket strip and tack together all round. Cut three 99cm

lengths of binding, press in half lengthways with upper folded half a little narrower than the other half. With narrower half of binding uppermost, insert the long top edge of each pocket into the binding and stitch in place.

3 Forming shoe pockets

Allowing 6mm at each end, mark out four pockets, each 12cm wide with 6cm

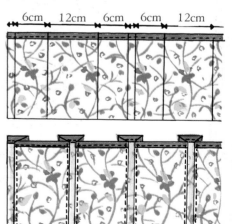

gussets and 6mm space between each pocket. Fold fabric to form pockets and press creases in place. Edge-stitch along the fold of each crease.

4 Binding lower edge of pockets
Pin top two rows of pockets down the folds to hold in formation. Unfold both edges of a length of binding and, with right sides facing and raw edges level, place binding along the lower edge of

Choose washable fabrics in contrasting light and dark patterns. Co-ordinate with your bedroom furnishings.

each pocket. Stitch along the fold line of binding. Fold the binding over to the inside.

5 Stitching shoe pockets

With wrong sides facing, tack the two main pieces together. Position pockets with right sides uppermost on the darker fabric side of the main piece as follows.

Place the pockets with the unfinished lower edge level with lower edge of main

piece and the other two rows of pockets with lower edge 5cm above top edge of previous pocket row. Pin in place.

Stitch the lower edges of the two top pocket rows to the main piece along the upper edge of binding. Stitch all round the main piece, 5mm from raw edges, enclosing lower edge of bottom pocket and side edges of all pocket pieces in the stitching. Stitch pockets to the main piece along the centre of the 6mm space between each pocket.

6 Attaching ribbon ties

Cut two 40cm lengths of ribbon and fold in half. With folds level with the raw edge, place the ribbon to the lower edge at the back of the main piece on the stitching lines between the outer and centre pockets.

7 Binding outer edge

Pin binding all round the outer edge in the same way as for the top edges of the pockets, joining ends of binding to fit and mitring corners. Pin, tack and stitch.

8 Finishing top edge

Fold 5cm over to the front along the top edge. Stitch in place along binding stitching line of top edge. Stitch again 2.5cm from top fold to form a channel for

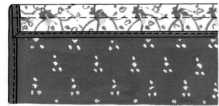

the dowelling. Paint the ends of the dowelling and slot into the channel. Cut 80cm of ribbon and tie one end round each end of the dowelling. Tuck loose ends of ribbon into the channel.

Making the stocking tidy

1 Binding pockets

In the same way as for the shoe tidy, bind the long top edges of all pockets. Press 5mm to the wrong side along the lower edges of the four upper pockets.

2 Stitching pockets

With right sides uppermost, arrange the pockets on the lighter main piece as follows: position the top pocket with top edge 10cm below top edge of main piece;

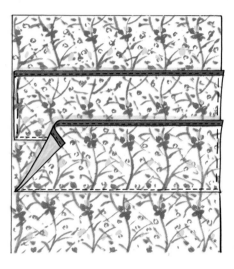

stitch across lower edge of pocket. Position the next pocket overlapping the lower edge of previous pocket so that the top edge is 10cm below top edge of previous pocket; stitch across lower edge. Stitch two more pockets in place in the same way. Use the pocket with the unpressed lower edge as the bottom pocket. Place the lower raw edge of this pocket level with the lower raw edge of main piece; pin and tack in place.

Tack main pieces together with wrong sides facing and enclosing the side edges of the pockets in the stitching. Place a

length of ribbon down the centre of the pockets. Stitch in place along both edges.

3 Attaching loops and tie

Cut two 6cm lengths of ribbon and fold to form loops. Position loops to line up with the ties at the lower edge of the shoe tidy.

With ends level with raw edge, tack loops to outer side at the top edge of the main piece.

Fold remaining ribbon in half and tack to the outer side at the centre of the lower edge so that the fold is level with the raw edge of main piece.

4 Finishing stocking tidy

Bind the outer edge in the same way as for the shoe tidy, enclosing ends of loops and the fold of ribbon tie in the binding.

Picnic set

Set the scene for an idyllic summer picnic with this pretty yet practical collection. The blanket is made from reversible quilted fabric to make sitting on the ground more comfortable, and it will easily seat four adults and a couple of small children. The blanket is about the

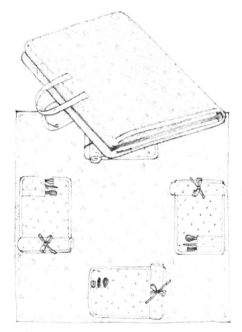

size of a double duvet so without the cloth it is ideal for lounging in the sun after lunch; and in the winter it will double as an attractive bed cover for a spare bed.

Use co-ordinating printed furnishing cottons for the quilted fabric, or buy it ready-made.

The place mats, also in quilted fabric, have pockets for cutlery and ribbon ties to hold the napkins in place. The mats are stitched to the central cloth so everything can be secured in place in advance. The cloth and napkins are made from co-ordinating prints to match either side of the quilted fabric. To pack the set, just fold the cloth and slip it inside the blanket, which folds up neatly into a bag with handles stitched to the underside.

Before you begin
Cotton prints are the most suitable fabrics to use for this set; choose two co-ordinating ones with contrasting backgrounds—use the darker side for the underside of the blanket and the tablecloth, and the lighter for the upper side of the blanket, the mats and the napkins.

To make life easier, you can buy reversible quilted fabric, which is available in a wide range of colours and patterns. Unquilted fabrics are normally available in the same designs.

Materials
For a blanket, about 2m square, and a cloth, about 1m square
☐ 4.60m × 120cm wide reversible quilted fabric for blanket and place mats
☐ 1.10m × 120cm wide fabric for cloth
☐ 1.40m × 120cm wide fabric for napkins, mat bindings and cutlery pockets.
☐ Matching sewing thread
☐ 2m × 1cm wide ribbon

Making-up instructions

1 Cutting out
For the blanket, cut two pieces 2m long from quilted fabric and trim each to 102cm wide; from the trimmed strips cut two handles 54cm × 9cm.

For the mats, cut four rectangles, 37cm × 25cm, from the remaining quilted fabric.

For the cloth, cut one 110cm square.

For the napkins, cut four 48cm squares; from the remaining fabric cut four cutlery pockets 9.5cm × 16cm, and 4cm wide bias strips to form four 130cm long strips when joined.

2 Joining blanket pieces
Thread your machine to match your contrasting fabrics, with one colour for the top thread and a contrasting colour for the bobbin thread.

With outsides together, stitch the blanket pieces together along one long edge 2cm in from the raw edges. Trim one seam allowance only to 1cm. With the inside uppermost, fold the trimmed

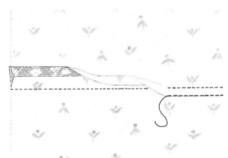

seam allowance over the trimmed edge, and pin the fold flat to the blanket so that both raw edges are enclosed. Stitch in place along the fold to form a double stitched seam.

3 Finishing the blanket edge
At the corners, press 1cm over to the inside. With outsides together, fold the corners with the pressed edges together and stitch across corners at right angles to the folded edge for 1.5cm to form mitres. Trim corners and turn right side

117

5 Making the handles
With outsides together, fold the handles in half lengthways and stitch the long edges together 1cm in from the raw edges. Turn right side out and press seams to centre of the back of handles.

With right sides of handles facing the bag, position one handle at each side of the top edge of the bag; pin in place with

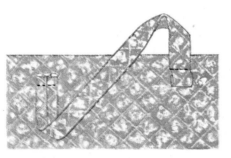

the outer edges of handles 20cm in from the sides of the bag and raw ends 4cm down from the top, so that the handles hang downwards. Unfold the blanket and stitch across 2cm from raw ends of handles. Fold the handles upwards and stitch again 3cm above the first stitching line so as to enclose the raw ends.

6 Making the cloth
Along two opposite edges, press a 5mm,

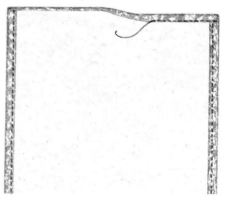

then a 2cm, hem to the wrong side and stitch in place. Make hems along the remaining two edges in the same way.

7 Making place mats
Along the top edge of each cutlery pocket, fold a 5mm, then a 1.5cm, hem to the wrong side and stitch in place. Press 1cm to wrong side along the right side edge of each pocket. Place the pockets to the lower left-hand corners of the mats with the side and lower edge level; pin in place. Stitch the right side edge of pocket to the mat, then stitch three more rows, each 2.5cm away from the previous row to form three individual pockets for the cutlery.

Trim the corners of the mats to curves. Join bias strips to form four 130cm lengths. With right sides together and raw edges level, pin the strips around the mats, easing the binding around the corners; join the ends of each strip to fit

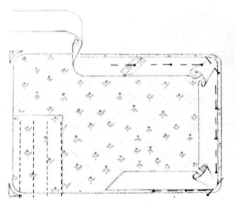

along a straight edge and complete pinning. Stitch in place 1cm from raw edges.

8 Finishing place mats
Fold the raw edges of the bias strip over to the wrong side of mat to form a binding. Pin the binding in place from the right

4 Folding the blanket
With the seam positioned across the blanket, fold one side edge over to two-thirds of the way across the blanket. Fold the opposite side over to meet the first fold. Fold top and bottom edges over to

out. Fold 1cm, then 1.5cm, to the inside around remaining side edges; pin and stitch in place.

meet the seam at the centre, then fold them again so that the seam is placed across the base of the resulting bag shape.

side of mat along the crease of the previous seam. Cut the ribbon into four 50cm lengths. Stitch centre of ribbon halfway down the right-hand edge of mat with two rows of stitching, one level with

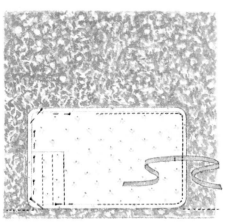

the binding seam and another 4cm away.

Position the mats on the cloth halfway along each side with the lower edge level with the inner edge of the cloth hem. Pin and stitch in place around the binding seamline so that the raw edges of the binding are enclosed behind the mat.

9 Making the napkins
Hem the napkins in the same way as the cloth, but make narrow hems by folding 5mm, then 5mm again, over to the wrong side.

10 Packing the picnic set
Fold the napkins in half widthways. Roll the napkins and tie to the side of mats with the ribbons. Place cutlery in the pockets. With right side inside, fold the cloth in three lengthways, then in three widthways so that the mats remain flat. Before folding the blanket, place the cloth at the centre and to one side of the seam so as to enclose it in the folded bag.

Index